solace

'One eye sees, the other feels'

Paul Klee

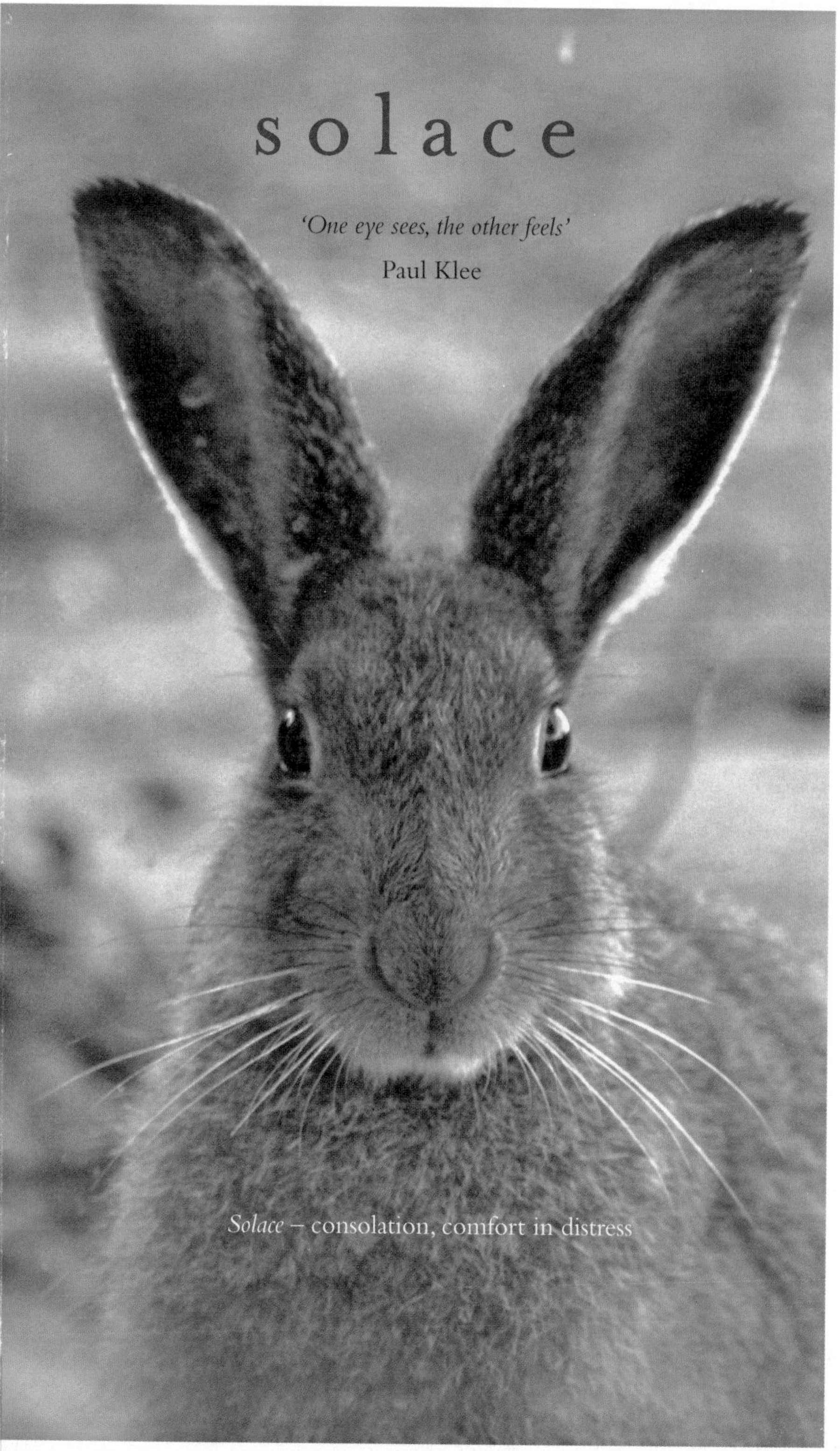

Solace – consolation, comfort in distress

Catherine Drea is a visual artist, writer and blogger who lives and works in rural County Waterford. Catherine writes a column called 'As I See It' for the *Waterford News & Star* and a blog on www.foxglovelane.com.

A graduate of National College of Art and Design (NCAD) and University College Cork (UCC), she has worked as a graphic designer, an art teacher and a group facilitator. In 1994 she co-founded Framework, a small charitable organisation, which supported community development and equality projects in Ireland. In 2010, after the economic crisis, Catherine and the Framework team began working from home. In 2011 she began to blog about Foxglove Lane, the small patch she calls home, and has won four Irish Blog Awards, including Best Photography Blog in 2018.

A lifelong activist, Catherine has been a campaigner in a number of social movements over the years. She remains a passionate advocate of equality, biodiversity and the natural world. She is currently Chairperson of the Waterford Healing Arts.

solace

Life, loss and the healing
power of nature

Catherine Drea

THE O'BRIEN PRESS
DUBLIN

First published 2022 by The O'Brien Press Ltd,
12 Terenure Road East, Rathgar, Dublin 6, D06 HD27, Ireland.
Tel: +353 1 4923333; Fax: +353 1 4922777
E-mail: books@obrien.ie
Website: obrien.ie
The O'Brien Press is a member of Publishing Ireland.

Enjoying life with O'BRIEN obrien.ie

ISBN: 978-1-78849-297-3

Illustrations, layout and design by Emma Byrne

10 9 8 7 6 5 4 3 2 1
27 26 25 24 23 22

Book cover: front image and back photograph by Catherine Drea; design by Emma Byrne

Printed and bound by Drukarnia Skleniarz, Poland.
The paper in this book is produced using pulp from managed forests.

Published in:
DUBLIN
UNESCO
City of Literature

ACKNOWLEDGEMENTS

Thanks to my beloved extended family, especially my Right-Hand Man, Alan O'Neill; my three much-loved sons, Evin, Dara and Fergal O'Neill; my sisters, Grace, Mary and Melanie Drea, who each have their own stories to tell, but who will always be at the centre of mine.

Thanks to my wonderful friends who walk around lakes, take a dip with me in the salty sea and the ones who have been there through thick and thin. To the workers and volunteers in community projects, family resource centres, and women's centres who I was so privileged to work with and be inspired by. To everyone connected with Framework, in particular Glynis Currie, our rock, who shared the ups and downs of joint leadership for more than twenty years. To my colleagues and friends in the Waterford Healing Arts who demonstrate every day the power of creativity and the solace it provides for the most vulnerable.

Thanks to the poets Róisín Sheehy, Joanne McCarthy and Mary Frances Ryan for their encouragement and for sharing their work. To the *Waterford News & Star* for giving me so much writing practice. To the Foxglove Lane Blog readers who have connected and supported me as part of such a positive online life and community.

Thanks to everyone in The O'Brien Press, in particular Nicola Reddy for thinking of me, Susan Houlden who so kindly supported me through the editing process and Emma Byrne for her intuitive book design.

Thanks to all who appear in photos including: Paul and Madeline Curran, Amy Hogan, Caroline Hennessey, Katriina Bent, Róisín Sheehy, Róisín O'Donovan, Alan O'Neill, Suzanna Crampton, Marie Drea Persson and Harry, and The Friday Morning Group at St Brigid's FRC.

Thanks to Grace Drea for her photo of Marie Drea Persson and Harry.

Thanks to the proud people of the Déise who protect the beauty and magic of County Waterford. Although we try to keep the secret of our haven of peace to ourselves, its serene beauty captivates everyone who gets out and explores our tracks and trails, the wild and deserted beaches, the magic road to the mountains. Home sweet home.

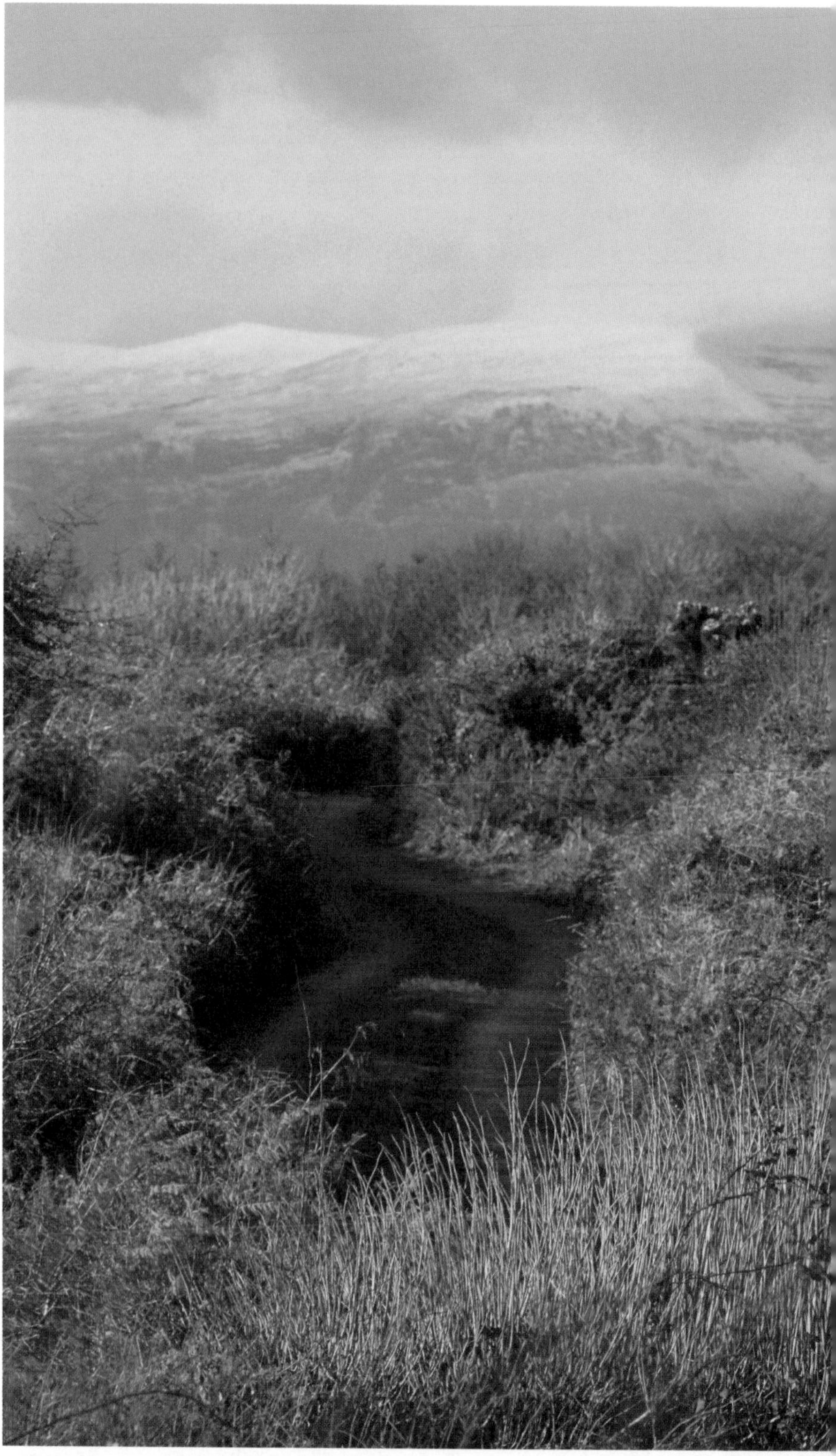

Contents

A word from
the author

We each seek out solace in our own way: in relationships of all kinds, in our families and the ones we love in spite of all the disappointments and failures, in a beloved dog or a cat, in a craft or skill that we hone over time, in art and music or in particular places on the Earth.

This book is about the path that led me to find solace in the simple goings on in the outer landscape, just beyond the threshold of my own back door. Solace is that feeling of calm and comfort, that sense of peace that is all around us when we are open to find it.

I have been lucky a few times in life when random doors of opportunity have opened and often it wasn't even a door I was knocking on. This time, right in the middle of a global pandemic, The O'Brien Press opened a door and invited me to take a peek inside. There, I caught a glimpse of a book with my name on it. That kid-in-a-sweet-shop moment proved to be totally irresistible, and although I didn't quite understand the full commitment the project would require, I dived in.

The complexity of a whole lifetime cannot fit into one book, but I hope that my solitary meanderings and writings about the landscape and tracks that I ramble in my small patch of the planet find some connection with yours. My inner child knew that solace was not as elusive as we might imagine, if only we took the time to notice. She was an expert in thriving in spite of grief, and knowing that love is the true solace that makes life worth living.

As I continued to put thoughts and images on paper, I rediscovered how my earliest childhood memories in the rose-petal garden and the present day in our wild couple of acres are deeply rooted in me; how the need to find a home and a place to feel safe was always fundamental to my sense of wellbeing, how persevering with a creative practice in times of turmoil has always brought solace to my days, how the joy of closeness to Mother Earth and mysteries that we all grapple with from time to time feed my imagination.

Whether you are on the city streets of New York or the dusty tracks of rural Turkey, I hope that you too can reawaken to the stories revealed in opening up to your patch of Mother Earth.

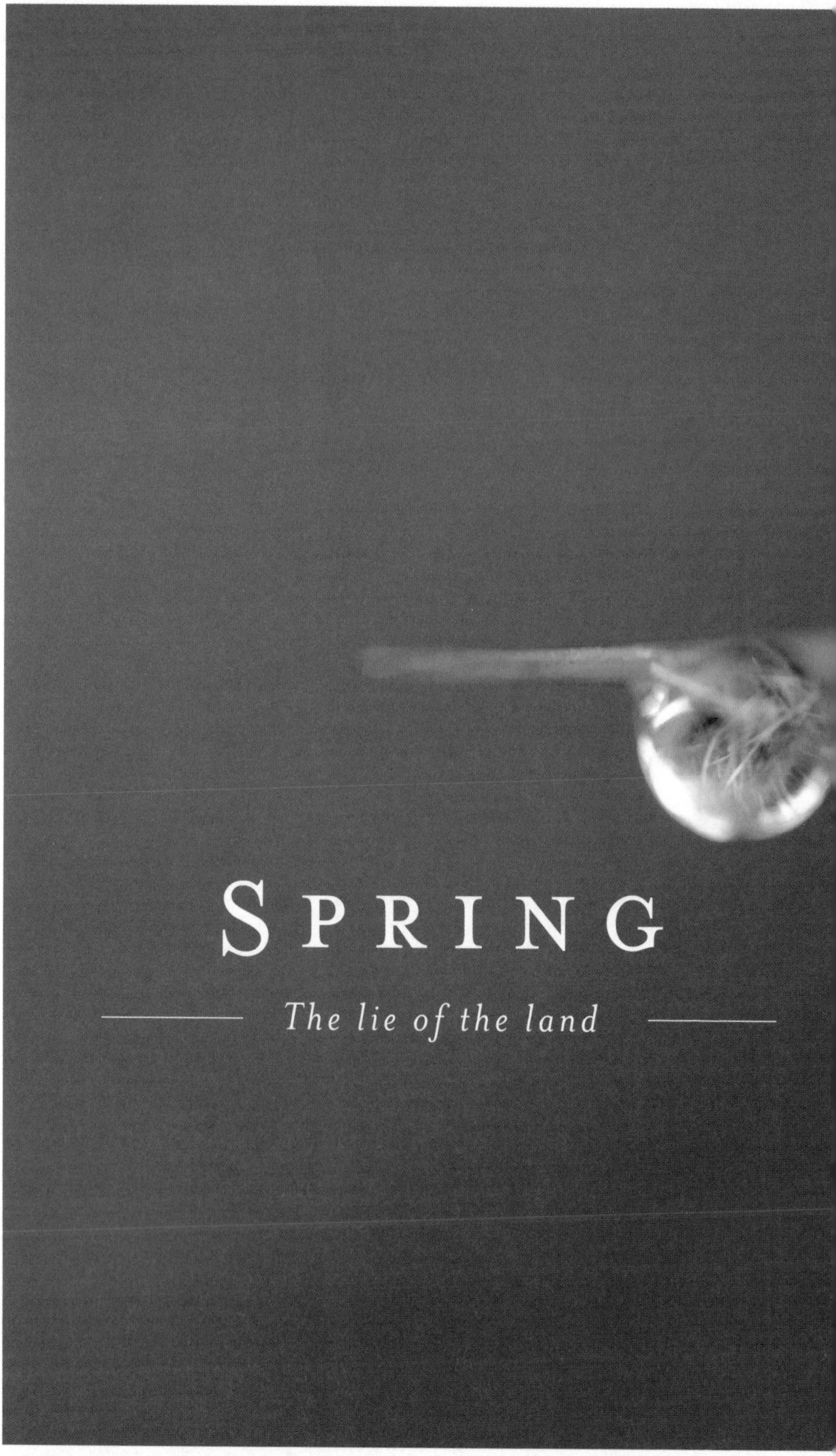

SPRING

The lie of the land

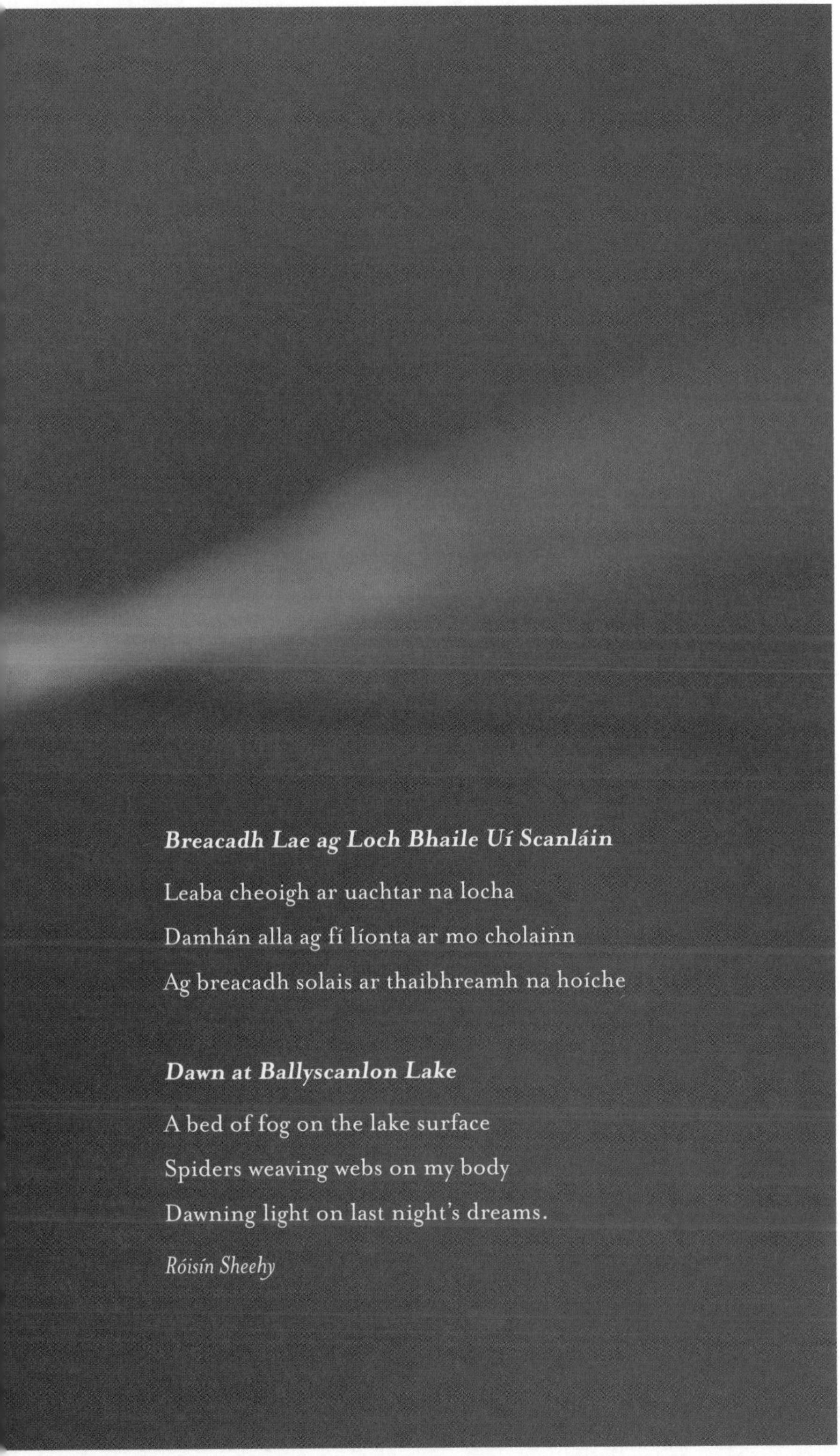

Breacadh Lae ag Loch Bhaile Uí Scanláin

Leaba cheoigh ar uachtar na locha
Damhán alla ag fí líonta ar mo cholainn
Ag breacadh solais ar thaibhreamh na hoíche

Dawn at Ballyscanlon Lake

A bed of fog on the lake surface
Spiders weaving webs on my body
Dawning light on last night's dreams.

Róisín Sheehy

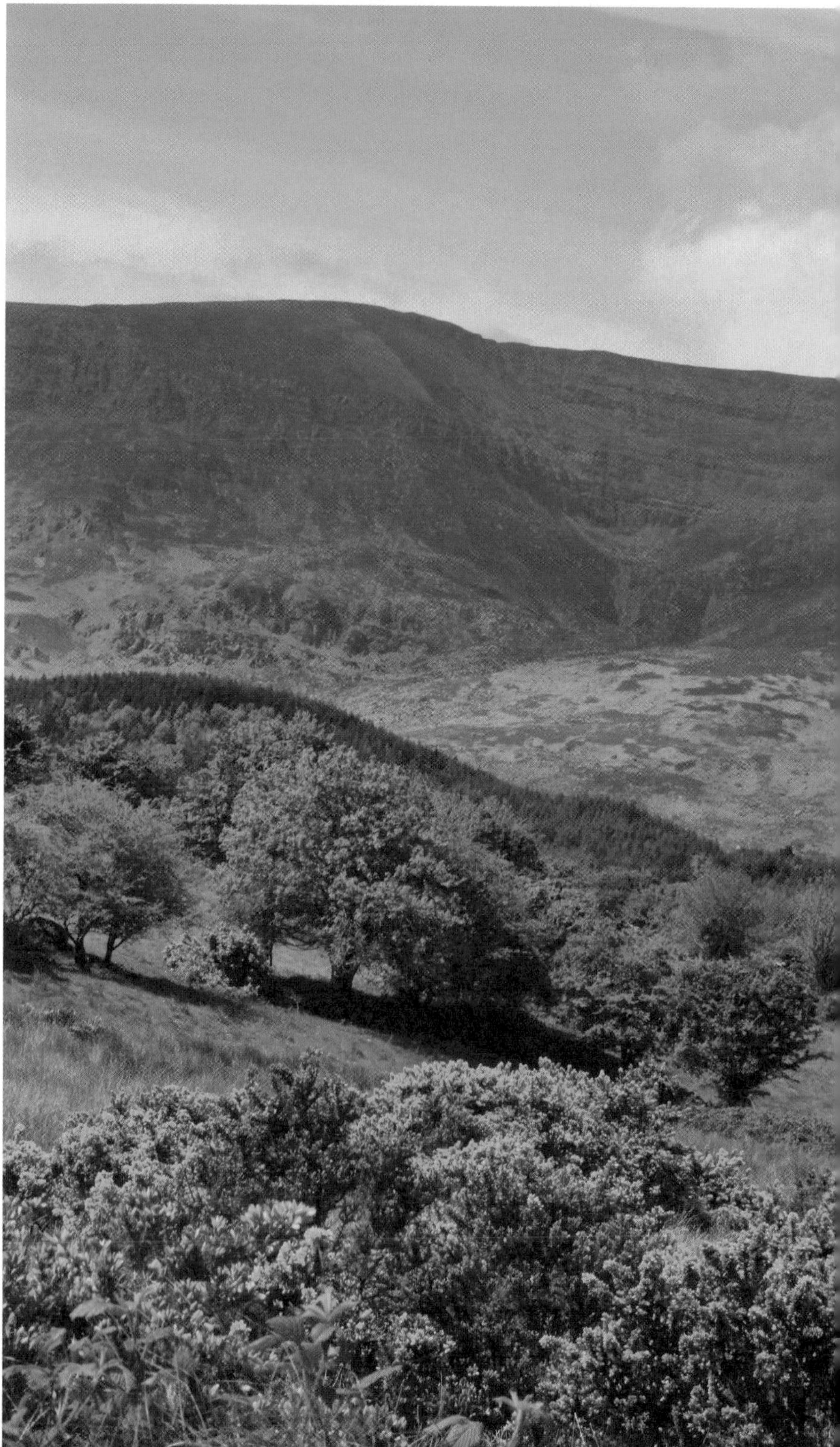

Chapter 1

Setting out

CROSSING THE THRESHOLD

In the beginning, I could have been walking anywhere for all the notice I took of what was happening around me. Although I have lived in rural Ireland for over forty years, setting out to walk the local lanes and tracks here was often just an escape from busyness and the pressures of work.

In 2010 after the economic crash my day to day life as a community support worker changed dramatically. To address sudden cutbacks in government funding, our office in the city closed its doors and from then on I began to work full-time from home. Home is here in a two-acre wild garden, beside a lake and about three kilometres from the coast. I live here with my Right-Hand Man, down a long boreen and far off the main road. Sometimes it feels like we live on an island and every so often we must let down the drawbridge to get back to the mainstream.

13

As a child, frequently moving house was part of my growing up. As a result, I was always looking for that elusive feeling of being home and grounded at last. During the late 1970s in Ireland, when most of our friends were emigrating, we had moved to the 'country' as an alternative adventure. First from Dublin to County Kilkenny, to live and work on a biodynamic farm and be part of a small, caring community. Then, on an outing to the sea one day we discovered the majesty of the Copper Coast in County Waterford and were smitten.

Just after the birth of our first son, my Right-Hand Man was offered a job as a lecturer in architecture at the local third-level college in Waterford. The following year, I also began teaching there in the Art Department. When my second son was born, as there was no maternity leave for part-time workers, we juggled childcare between us and there were many stolen moments running out to feed the baby in the back of the car or swopping parenting roles in the carpark.

Having renovated an old cottage, where our third son was born, we experienced the 'built in obsolescence' of old buildings and decided to move to an even quieter spot and build a new house. We had lived in the cottage with the three boys as we built on top, around and inside of it. After almost twenty years, and as the boys became young adults, we built that new house and set about turning a boggy field into a habitat-friendly wilderness.

We both left our jobs in the college in the early 1990s and set up organisations to address some of the new work that was required after Ireland received substantial funds for equality from the EU. My work was focussed on supporting small local communities tackling unacceptable levels of poverty, while his was leading a gender-focussed project exploring men's development and the needs in particular of disadvantaged men. For the rest of our working lives these absorbing jobs took us travelling around Ireland; rural Waterford was the place we returned to for respite.

After many years of sustained work by a lot of people, marginalised communities in Ireland were starting to thrive again. Then suddenly came the shock of the economic crisis in 2008. Without doubt there was a kind of grief in Ireland at what was about to be lost. My own work team were all now working from home, thrown into unforeseen chaos. The small non-profit set up by myself and my good friend, an art therapist, had been friendly and fostered belonging. In this new situation of working from home, I immediately missed the community of women who had become like a second family. How was I going to deal with the loneliness and isolation of this new life? I could literally go for days without bumping into anyone around here.

Gradually, having absolutely no choice in the matter, I accepted the limitations of the working-from-home lifestyle, adapted to the new situation, put my desk at a window and settled in all over again. As I write this, the memories of disorientation and loss are only intensified by the Covid-19 pandemic, with the sudden and shocking instructions for the whole country to stay at home. As the various lockdowns were called throughout the pandemic, I was reminded of how I had already crossed a threshold onto a well-worn path of trying to find solace in long days alone, a shrinking terrain and an unsteady future.

Opening up space

Both after the economic crash and with the arrival of the pandemic, it became obvious that working from home, I would need to get out of the house every day and the only option open to me was to have a solo walk around this small patch of the world. Maybe walking could create a lifeline to the kind of normality that I was used to?

In the 1990s and early 2000s, I had so loved commuting to the city, having lunch with friends and gossiping in the street with anyone I met. After the changes brought on by the economic crash in 2008 I found myself housebound for

days on end; as for many in the days of the pandemic, the crucial thing then was for me to get a change of view and find a way to experience the day outside of myself.

We bring our whole selves with us when we walk. Sometimes we have bad days with brooding moods or we are full of sunshine and hope. The land is not embroiled in our inner life and although I could grasp that, my heart was often heavy on these walks.

The inner voices chattered away too, prattling on about the shock of it all and how we would solve the problems of our shrinking budgets and our growing workload. The narratives in our heads, these voices that insist on trying to monitor us through life, can be somewhat quieted by bringing our attention to the wonders of being alive, healthy and at least temporarily able-bodied. But at that time, any or all of these moods could overwhelm me on these lonely walks.

The landscape opened up space, but in the beginning it felt like too much space. The preoccupations of surviving the economic crash and how it would all be resolved weighed heavily. Walking alone initially didn't offer any solutions or provide directions for the future either. It was fresh air, a break from the computer and exercise.

Only the distraction of my neighbour Lena's dogs and how they amused her would help to lift my spirits as we chatted on the lane. She had grown up here, lived alone with her animals and knew the land and the seasons better than anyone. We were the same age and although we had lived very different lives, I like to think we connected in a special way, chatting about the weather and everyday life. Sharing these quiet moments meant a lot to both of us.

Other than that, the slow pace of my new life and the daily walks into the blur of the familiar did nothing to inspire me as I trudged in all weathers. It got me out of the house, but that was all.

RECLAIMING CURIOSITY

On these walks I began to notice birds, but as yet didn't know many of their habits as I do now. When I was out in the early mornings I kneeled down to explore spiders' webs laden with dew. Coming from a family phobic about spiders, the beauty and artistry of web creation was a revelation! On icy days I saw that the vegetation sparkled with dew crystals like exotic lace.

Over time, I became more curious about the names of plants, trees, animals and birds around here. It wasn't so

much that I needed to know their proper names, it was so that I could understand more the uniqueness of each in front of my eyes — the feathers and colours of birds, the petal shapes and stamens of flowers, the outline of leaves. Now, if a new species appears I will spot it instantly and probably learn and forget its proper name in no time too!

The loneliness I had initially feared was very different to this new kind of aloneness. Slowly my attention began to shift from the inner voices of despair to an outer curiosity about this place. My head came up, my eyes opened wider, my ears became more sensitive. In these daily walks with no one but my re-emerging inner child, I began to notice a growing calm, and an awakening of my senses.

Not since I was a very small girl, alone in a small back garden, had I felt deeply held in the world. I began to recognise an old feeling of belonging to the land, this beautiful country and our planet. Maybe it's not so much where you are, as how you are? It's not so much walking in a place of beauty, as it is finding beauty in the place where you walk.

Noticing the wonder of the everyday slowly reawakened my urge to care and fired my creativity in a new way. Finding solace in nature and the everyday nurtured me at this time when I felt quite lost.

Upheaval

In those years after the economic crash, when everything was so uncertain and bleak, there was another upheaval going

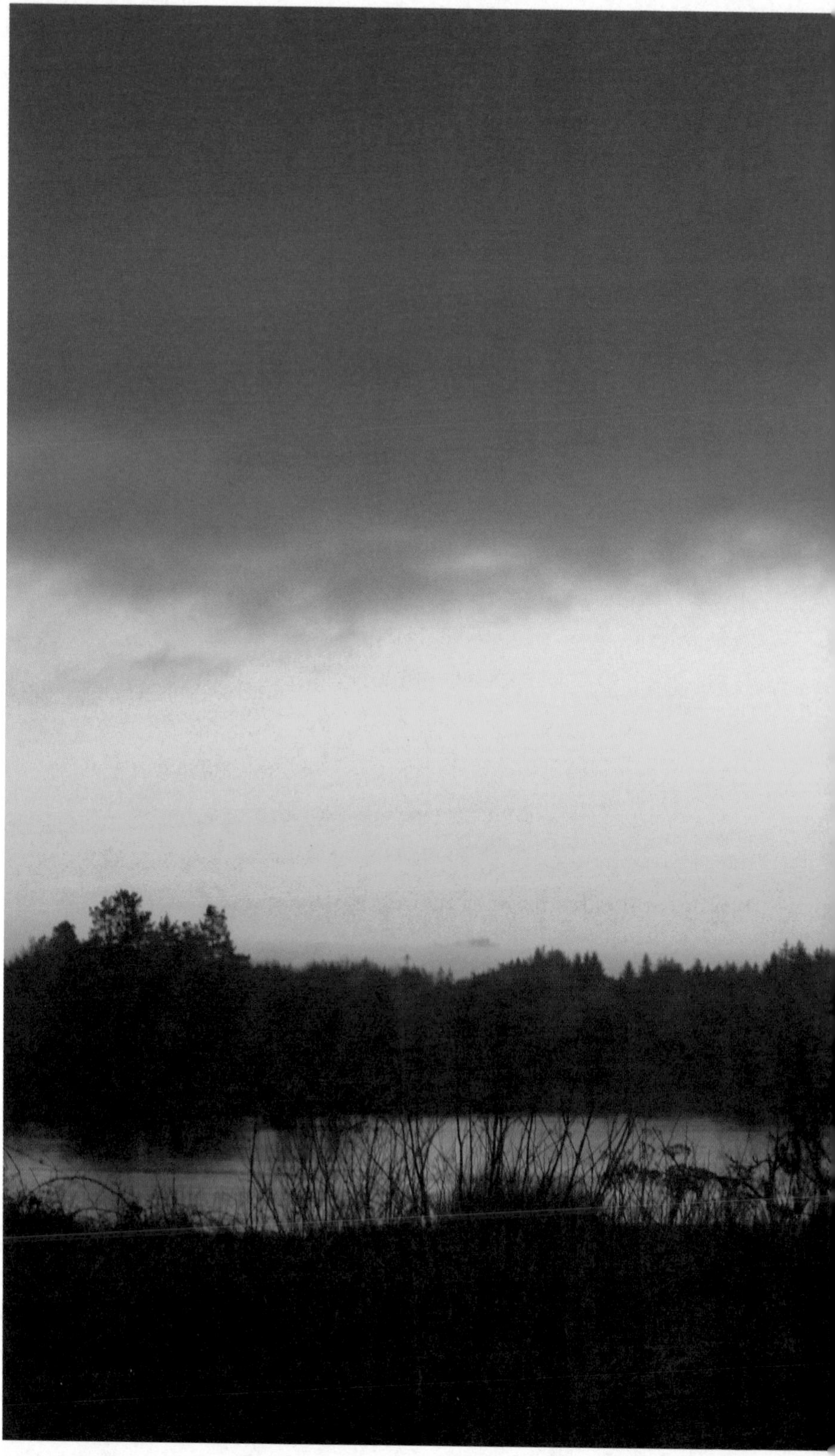

on as my dear old dad was in the final part of his life. I was spending weekends travelling to the other end of the country to spend time with him and support his care. He was very clear about how he wanted to die and he often gripped my hand and repeated it, making sure that his wishes were understood. He wanted to die at home, no ifs or buts. Knowing what he wanted, and going through that last year with him, I was never more acutely aware of the preciousness of being alive and healthy.

Coming out of that winter with Dad I was intensely aware of the joy of light, the magic of crisp mornings underfoot, the rich tones of sunsets over the lake. Death was all around me and yet, there was an exquisite beauty in it.

Dad noticed the beauty of the living world too when by a macabre coincidence we used to take him in a wheelchair on a ramble up to the graveyard where he would eventually be laid to rest. Starting out fairly cranky about the whole idea, he would, in spite of his blindness, begin to notice shadows, light, colour, scents and sounds. He still had a deep connection to nature, responding with a sigh or a chuckle when he recognised a dog passing or a colourful display of leaves.

Slowing down and taking more time to relax in the moment helped me to stay more present with Dad. Being with him in those last months was more a matter of sitting in listening mode or even in complete silence. Just to wake up in the morning was a bonus for Dad, as he used to say regularly. Breakfast with him was a pleasure as he would hum with happiness just because he was 'still here'.

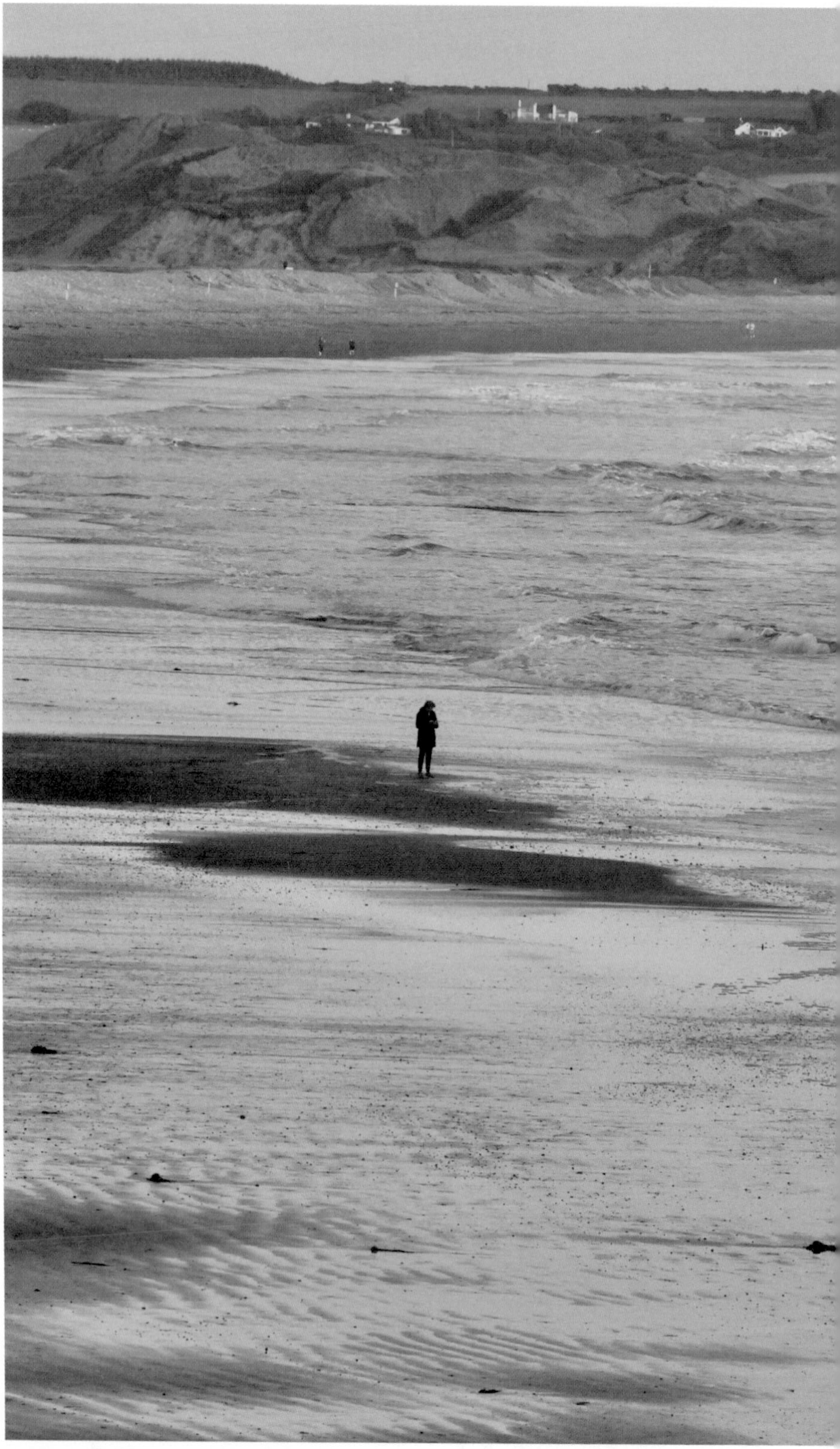

Chapter 2

This landscape

THE TRACKS AND TRAILS

A s I slowed my pace on these solo walks, the outer landscape began to reveal her many hidden treasures. The immediate surface layer of the land balanced my attention between observing the material world and having a holiday from my inner turmoil. Long before drones became fashionable, the layers of the landscape absorbed part of me as I imagined helicopter views – rolling countryside, distant mountains, two small lakes and meandering country roads down to the coast.

When my three sons were small I used to wheel a big, old pram around the country lanes. The youngest would be wrapped up in knits and blankets, while the older two ran on ahead foraging or finding small creatures in the ditches. We

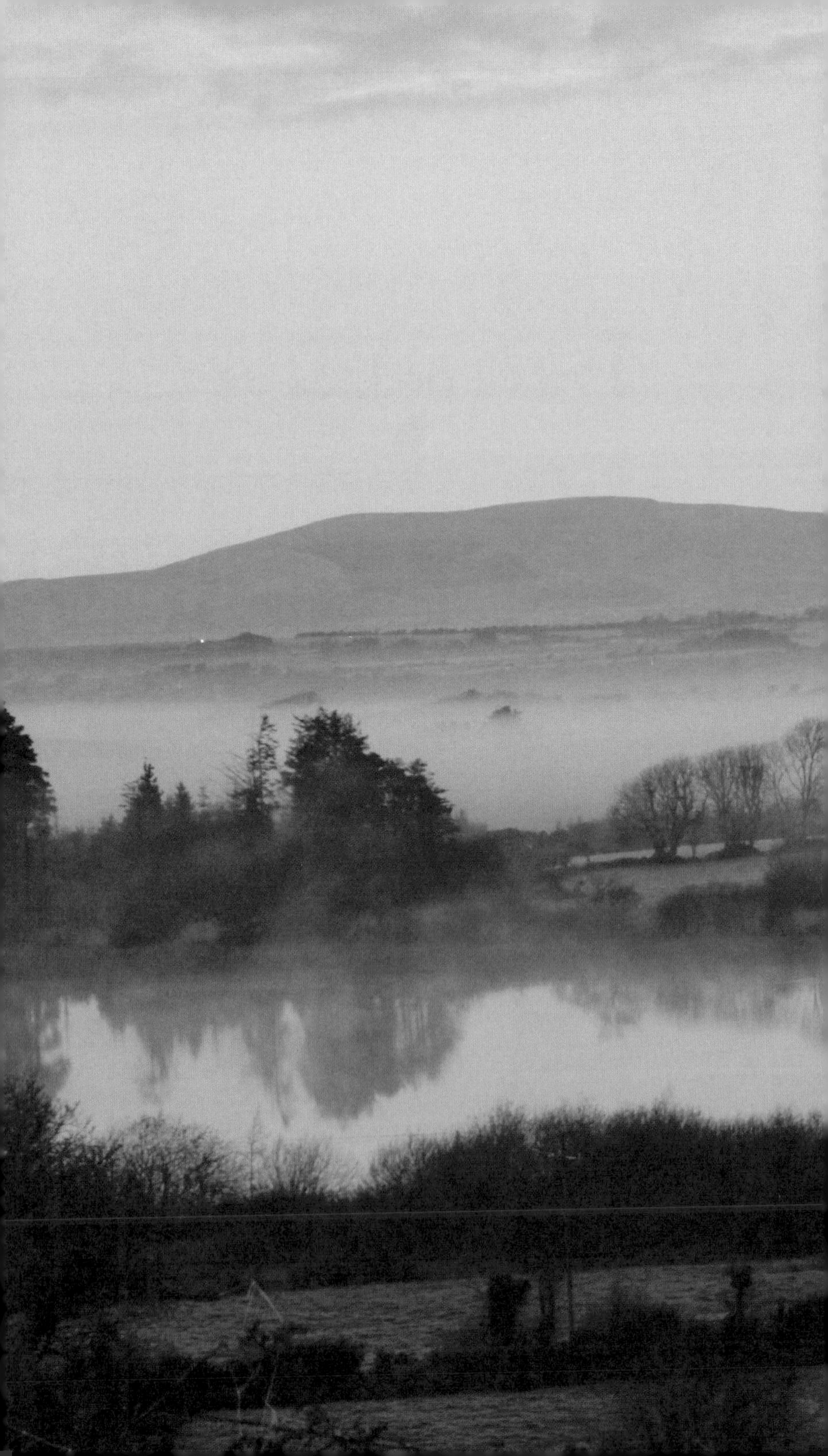

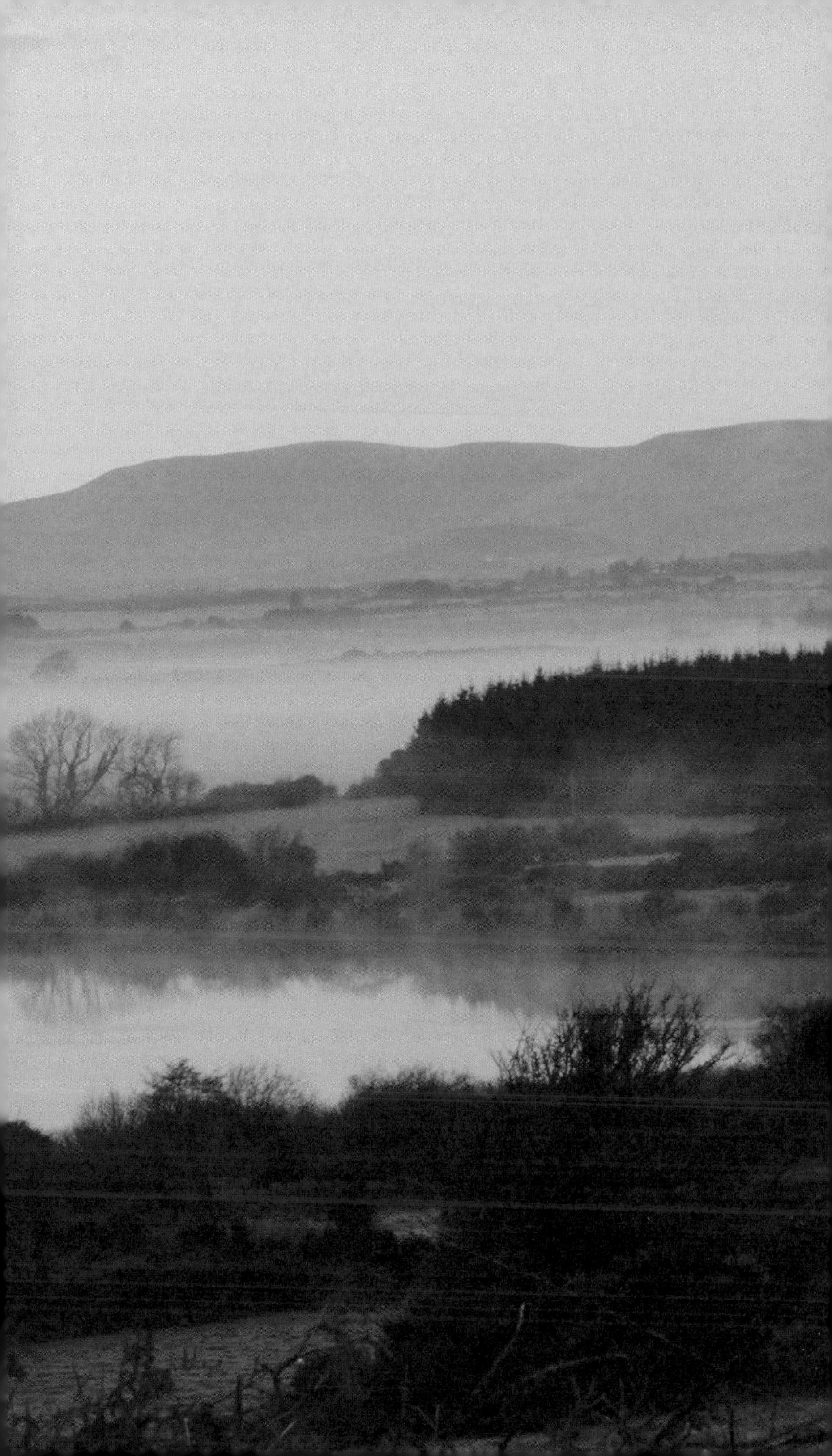

used to cross the yard of a deserted farm house and the boys would entertain me with tales of ghosts and ghouls that they imagined dwelt there. Their little legs would hop and skip along until one or other would tire and I would heap them up on top of the baby and speed off home — a stagecoach full of giggling boys.

Now I am imagining that if you were walking with me here, we would first figure out our options as to which layers, routes and destinations to explore together. We could begin at the top of our lane with a spectacular view to the Comeragh Mountains all the way across the soft hilly farmland of County Waterford. This view takes in the direction of the new Waterford Greenway, which follows an old railway track all the way west to Dungarvan. Here we would pass standing stones, including a spectacular dolmen, and eventually connect to the meandering river Suir.

Alternatively, we could wander through quaint lanes and trails that lead down to the sea. In one direction we could go through the Anne Valley from Dunhill, past the ruins of a Norman castle and through the wetlands all the way to Annestown Beach.

In the other direction, we would have a seven kilometre downhill stroll into Tramore, a sunny South East holiday resort. Beloved of generations of holiday makers, *Trá Mhór* means the Great Beach and it is the classic spectacular golden beach of everyone's fantasies.

For a shorter walk we could ramble through grassy meadows to the lake or follow a boreen to an abandoned reservoir.

Here, we would pass another deserted house and walk through a farmyard with a thatched cottage and a gaggle of noisy geese. This is a gentle landscape, typical of many off-the-beaten tracks in Ireland. On your first walk here, like me, you might find yourself chatting away about how beautiful it is, enjoying the green views and twisty lanes.

Although just typical country lanes, I imagine that these tracks once made well-worn paths for our ancestors. Many of the ancient stones standing abandoned in the middle of ploughed fields or strewn across farms and forests were once sites of the earliest community life on this land. In Ireland this is probably true of many places, but here the tracks are not much walked except by locals and so have remained old.

Little did any of us know that during a pandemic as yet unheard of, we would be limited to only two kilometres of walking. At least by then I would be well rehearsed and would know the landscape like the back of my hand. I would also have developed a few of the coping skills and the resilience needed for isolation and falling back on your own resources.

THE ANCESTORS AT CNOC AN CHAILLIGHE

Between here and the road to the Comeragh Mountains is the at least four-thousand-year-old Gaulstown Dolmen, a portal tomb of huge stones set in a peaceful grove of oaks. Our earliest ancestors must have been mindful of its positioning. The site is named for the townland, but is situated

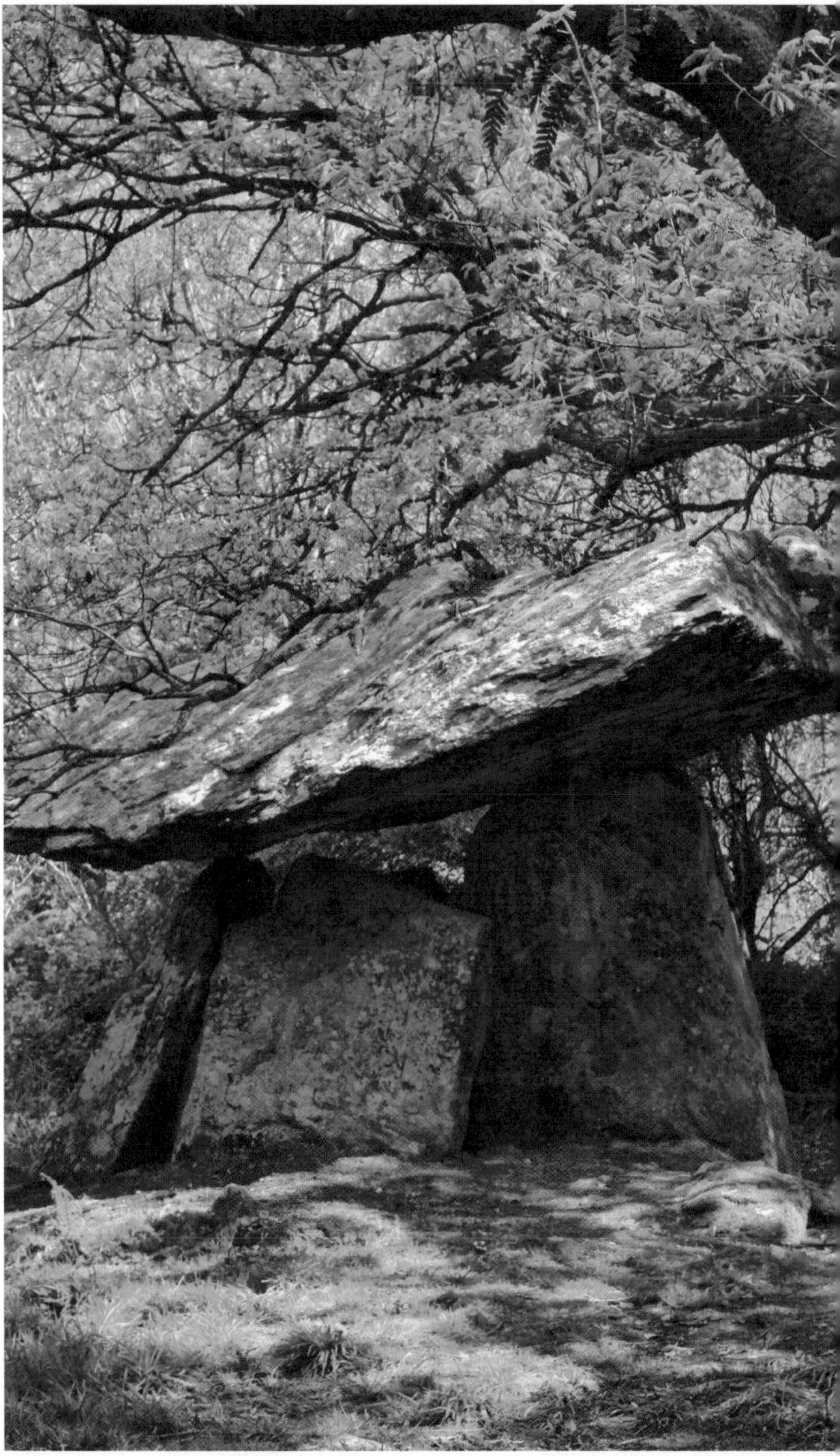

at the foot of Cnoc an Chaillighe, or Hill of the Hag, something that I enjoy as more significant.

An Cailleach, the old woman, the hag, or the crone, is found
in many cultures around the world. In some stories she can
be found weaving a tapestry of the world, creating dark spells
for those who plunder the Earth or lying in wait to punish
hunters who are all take and no give. This sacred place at the
foot of the Hill of the Hag still resonates with women and I
once circle-danced here with a group of them at the winter
solstice.

Along the small road to the dolmen is a fully grown hawthorn hedgerow. Hawthorns are an ancient native tree and
often remind me of the craggy olive trees of the Mediter-
ranean that live for hundreds of years. It is rare to see a full
hedgerow like this as fences have replaced many of these
corridors of life and beauty. In spring these hawthorn trees

reward us with a dome of blossoms and in winter with the red haws that the birds love so much.

Here, in this ancient place, it is easy to imagine an assortment of souls, meandering there like us. Perhaps the foragers of old rambled these lanes thinking about the big questions and the cycles of life as we do too. I think of them along these tracks and trails, wondering where their memory is most present. What were the women's lives like and did they pick blackberries and crab apples along the lanes just like we do on summer evenings?

UNDERFOOT

As I walked these paths on a daily basis the anxiety about work and my future faded into the background and my utter insignificance grew. My attention was being absorbed by the beauty and the richness of the landscape and I began to feel more and more like a tiny ant on the back of a huge beast.

One day while flying from Waterford Airport to Galway I was scanning all the places I knew down below: Tramore, the great beach, the coastline towards the west and Dungarvan. Suddenly I found that the plane was turning over the hills and lakes of my own place. It was clear that the land around here forms a significant bowl shape in the landscape. I could see the geological past of my patch being expressed as a huge, soft sculpture of earth.

That day I could see the lake at the centre of my world, which I had been told once was the crater of an ancient

volcano. It is still surrounded by a large rim of rocks and hills. I often sense these curves. Maybe someday from a boat in the middle of the lake, or when swimming out there, you can look around and get a sense of its shape too – a crater held by a circle of land, millions of years old and ninety metres deep at its centre.

In and around the wildest parts of the lake there are small fish, dragonflies, scented mint and ground-nesting birds. By stealth, I have encountered badgers, foxes and rabbits there, but my favourite resident animal is the mythological shape-shifting Irish hare. Hares are usually safely hidden during the day and it is at night that you will catch sight of these animal residents. They are easiest to spot when they are trundling home in the early hours after a hard night.

To this day, I send my sons regular photos of animal activity here. They still ooh and aah when I capture a visit from the jaunty badgers on the webcam. Growing up they kept mice, gerbils and guinea pigs in the house, and in their pockets. An assortment of cats, dogs and birds lived in their rooms. One cat gave birth on top of my eldest son as he slept, while another set of kittens, brought into the house by a neighbour's marmalade tomcat, were christened John and Jesus. The boys were close to animals in a way that I never was as a child and their ease and delight was contagious to someone who only ever had one pet tortoise that passed away during its first winter hibernation.

If you walk here you too will become more aware of animals and the paths they follow. You won't necessarily meet any, but their presence will be felt, in the long grass, in their tracks across boundaries and the burrows they make through ditches and hedgerows. Underfoot you are treading on the silent routes of our companion species. We and they know the land in our own animal way.

LETTING GO

My dad declined further and in the end he got his wish to die at home surrounded by his family, just as the sun was going down. Every year on that date, I go to the edge of the lake or back to the dolmen and watch the sun setting. I think of Dad and the many mysteries of letting go, looking for solace in times of grief.

For the wake we dressed Dad up in his favourite geansaí. At an early age he had shown great promise as a golfer and for many years had a 'scratch' handicap. Never was he jollier

than on a golf course, dressed in a multicoloured sweater and a flat cap, out playing with his mates of all ages. Ever since the day I whacked my younger sister in the head with a golf club on the golfing range, none of his four daughters were ever encouraged to set foot on a golf course. To this day none of us have any interest in it. Although I probably should have put golfing paraphernalia into his coffin, instead I put four tiny photographs I had taken of colourful butterflies.

That spring, time became filtered through a growing awareness of our 365-day journey around the sun – of our little planet, spinning through the universe once every year, turning towards the light – and how the cycles of the years were becoming a rhythm in my life.

In the months that followed I was startled by tiny wildflowers, mosses, grasses, lichens and the insects who lived on them. The colour changes in spring from the palest primroses on the ditches to the bright blue of scented bluebells and then the spectacular cerise of summer foxgloves appearing in swathes on the lanes and hills delighted my senses. Somehow the rawness of grief made everything sing.

From then on, I began to appreciate this landscape and my place in it all the more.

If I had put a sign over my desk in those early months of dealing with the loss of my dad, it might have read, 'We are here, we are alive and every moment counts.'

The natural world outside my own door and the small details of everyday life gradually helped to restore my senses, but it also woke up a fierce new love of living.

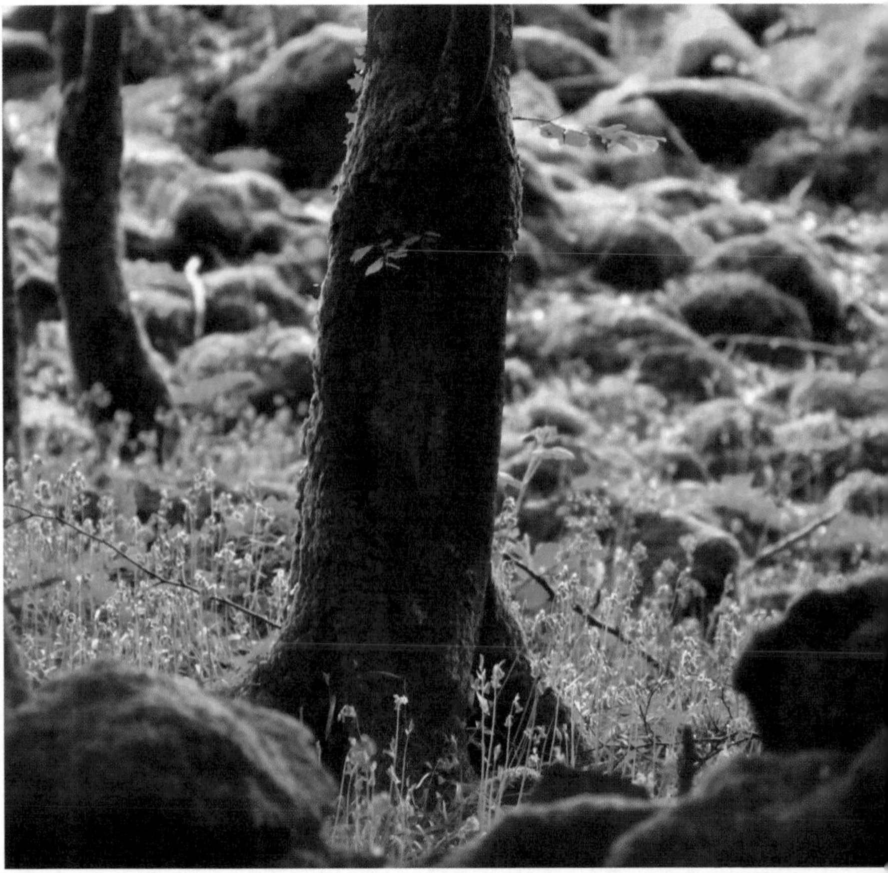

Chapter 3

When spring comes

UNFURLING

Spring is simply impossible to resist. The first greens are bright and bursting with possibilities, appearing in the most unlikely places. Light creeps back into our days.

During the first long, long winter of the pandemic, every day and many times a day, I checked the trees for leaves. The weather seemed colder than normal and even the buds were reluctant to risk that unseasonal nip in the air. Did we ever experience the changing seasons with such intensity?

In my earlier days, after the sudden lifestyle changes of the economic crash, ditches and hedgerows slowly began to intrigue me. Many of them had been covered up with mosses and it seemed as if the vegetation had lain largely undisturbed for generations. The old trees within these hedgerows had powerful girth and height and were swaddled in ivy and moss. Under the shade of these trees a heavenly

scent brought my attention to bluebells growing amongst white stitchwort, bringing back early memories of woodland adventures.

I would dilly-dally for ages, looking at small details: green unfurling ferns, unravelling buds on willow trees and the beginnings of foxgloves. Looking, seeing, learning about the tiny and the miraculous.

As spring unfurls each year the new season's buttercups are like exotic jewels. Each thread in the hedgerow weaves into being in its own time, part of the whole. Under the trees, where drifts of violets are tangled, there are mists of blue and green with the odd splash of pink from herb-Robert or creeping vetch.

Spring is a time for a deliberate and slow opening. Along these hedgerows and lanes, before the grass is too long or the leaves are too dark green, there is unadulterated optimism and joy. Spring comes. No matter what age we are or what is going on in the world we know that spring returns; she always does.

In those early days of grieving the death of my dad, spring helped to heal my loss and reminded me of the privilege of our short time on this planet. The more I immersed myself in the nature surrounding me, the more I cared about it all: the wonder and variety of birdsong, the dark, dappled caves of woodland, the cool balm of a freshwater lake. It was a mixed blessing indulging in the extraordinary beauty of the world and at the same time becoming more fearful for the loss of it.

BLOSSOMING

Daily walking with attention began to be a regular practice. One day I came across a ditch full of the humble blackthorn

blossom. These trees are one of the first to bloom and their creamy blossoms bud on dark branches. 'Blackthorn: flowers before leaves, hawthorn: leaves before flowers.'

Surely I had seen these trees before? They were in front of me all my life. I stood beneath them transfixed by these tiny white flowers and although I couldn't pick them, eat them or capture their beauty in any way, this moment filled my being. Nothing else intruded on the complete perfection of that flower.

Blackthorn blossoms are so utterly pure in design. The contrast of hundreds of white blossoms against dark branches is unique in our hedgerows of overwhelming greens and lush vegetation. I had known this useful native tree only for the sloes it produces in winter, which make a Christmassy red sloe gin. But in the intensity of grief, which for some reason heightened my experience of that particular spring, blackthorn blossom drew me into an obsessional delight.

That year as spring marched on and the hawthorn blossoms appeared on the faery tree I found myself bouncing out of bed with a renewed energy to photograph them in this light or that. I examined closely the inner workings of the flower. As it became tinged with pink at the turning of the season, I was simply besotted.

From then on I would look out for blackthorn and hawthorn every year. Something had significantly changed about how I saw the world after that.

THE INNER CHILD

Gradually I noticed that my inner child had come along for these walks too. Our inner child can stay with us through life and strangely becomes more present as we age; often we find ourselves drawn towards wonder and less to striving. My inner child reminded me of lingering wordless memories, a time when everything was play. She had a more trusting and spontaneous response to the world than grown-up me.

My inner child was a being of boundless imagination as well as the bearer of vulnerability, hurt and sensitivity. She had very strong emotional attachments; bonds and memories that could not always be explained. My inner child had never truly felt a sense of belonging; now released into the wild, she was remembering that time before the grief.

A friend to faeries, sprites and giants, this inner child did not always make much sense to the 'adult in the room' and

could create all sorts of misunderstandings or unreasonable demands. A longing for freedom and less responsibility settled into my body at a deep level and soon I would give up my day job completely as a result of her nagging. Locked up and suppressed for far too long, the inner child was looking for a bit more rope.

It was going to be a battle royal to find out how to keep a balance between the pair of us. Having spent years perfecting a good version of a grown-up, it seemed now that I was to be reduced to a very simple co-existence. On one level a worldly activist in my job and on the other a girl seeking the cute and the cuddly, talking to robins, bees and herself.

I began to remember that there was a place to go back to where I had felt fully myself and safely held in the world. It was somewhere I went all the time without even knowing how. It was a place that allowed me to nourish an inner introvert while at the same time demonstrate to the world a well-adjusted gregarious type. Over many years the pretence had begun to fade. But at least I maintained the pretence to myself that I was getting away with it!

THE GREAT MOTHER

This memory of being safe and held soothed some anxiety about the world and the future. While I was present in nature, preoccupied in capturing it with my lens, I felt sure I was experiencing what our ancestors called the 'Great Mother'. This is the Earth as Mother, worshipped by ancient civilisations, part myth, part intuition, part folk memory, but a wonderful metaphor for life-giving and preservation. Seeing nature as birthing-Mother energy was for me a way of entering into the mysteries of the living world that rational language couldn't express adequately.

By connecting with this concept of the Mother in nature, it came back to me, that I had first experienced this with my own mother, Addie, in our small back garden. The scant memories and yet the deep physical connection with her were where the inner landscape and the outer world had first met for me as a young child. The feeling of being held and safe in nature were similar to that sense of being home.

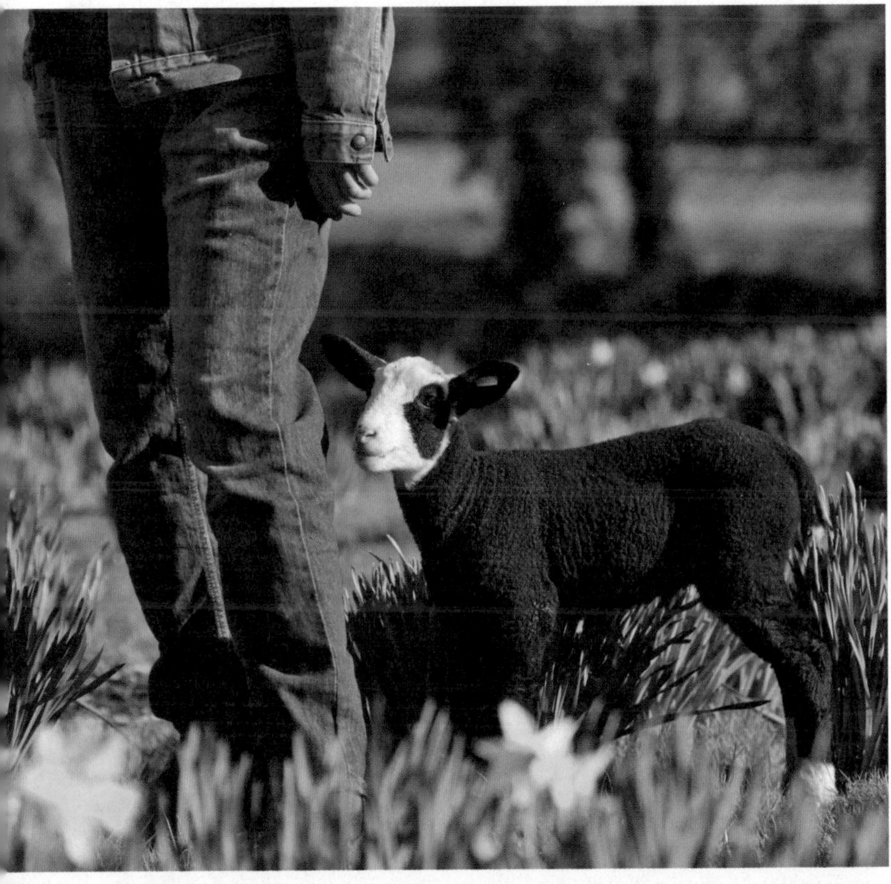

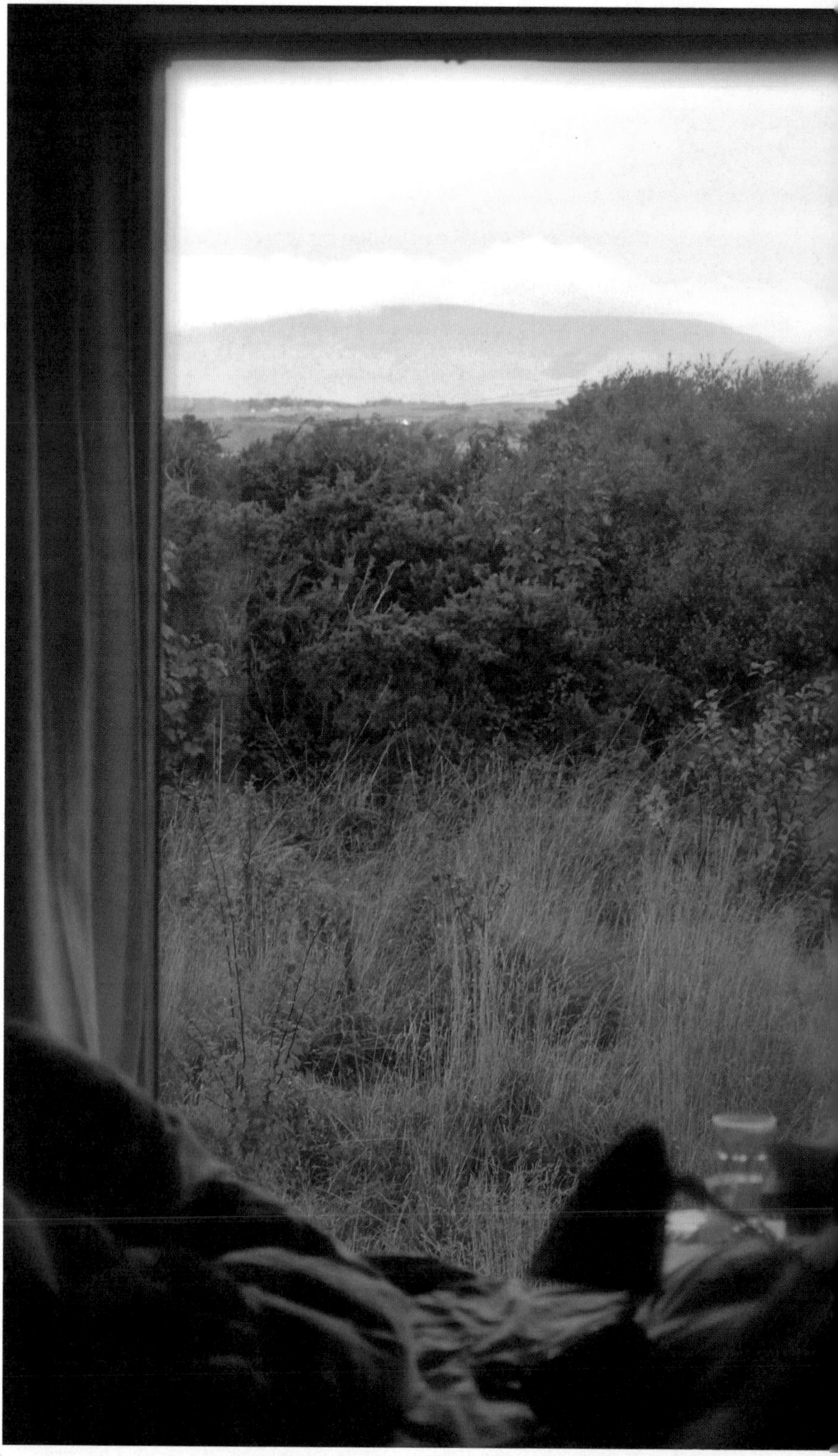

Chapter 4

Nesting

HOME

Anywhere we find ourselves can become home, but this particular few acres where I now live is one I feel deeply rooted in. It may be because by the time I arrived here I had lived in fourteen different homes, five of them before the age of ten.

On our walk here together you would probably spot my house a mile off because of the untidy mess of trees, brambles and nettles that thrive here! The dream was to live in a peaceful place, surrounded by nature and as far away as possible from the busyness of modern life. An architect and an artist would surely want to have a go at building their own home and this piece of land gave us that lucky opportunity.

There is no doubt that building random houses in rural Ireland has impacted negatively on the environment. Human activity is the main cause of the destruction of Ireland's biodiversity, so although guilty as charged, I try to do my bit for nature and give something back. This mess of under-growth and 'weeds' that the more progressive call 'rewilding' is part of that effort.

The plan here was to minimise our impact on the land by creating a sanctuary for the remaining wildlife and bio-diversity. We like to think that, in spite of the destruction of Ireland's wild places, it is still possible to support some balance between human, animal and plant welfare. When I discovered that the Greek 'oikos' means home, and it's from this that the English word 'ecology' is formed, it completed the picture.

On the first night after moving into the unfinished house, the silence was deafening. I listened hard to hear anything familiar, anything that might steady my complete disorientation. In the silence there was stillness, but no discernible sound. To the north of the land where we built the house dozens of families had lived in pre-famine times. There is no trace of their existence now, just a whisper in the imagination.

I listened hard, as you do when you are apprehensive. During that first night I kept getting up and wandering to the window on the half-built second floor. Surrounded by everything we owned piled up in boxes, at five o'clock I was still awake. With no curtains, the moon's silvery light cast long shadows across the floor.

I looked out again and again, overwhelmed by the new view, one that I now know so well. In the moonlight, just below me, on a patch of gravel, I saw a flicker of movement. For the first time in my life I then saw a hare and three leverets. The mother sat there in contemplation while the young hopped around her. Unaware of my presence, it was as if I was intruding on their patch. And so I was.

An elusive creature

The Irish hare is an elusive creature. I had only ever seen one caught in the headlights of the car or on the old Irish threepenny piece. Celtic mythology portrays the hare as a shape-shifting goddess, with the power to disguise herself in a hare's body. To me, in the magical moonlight of my first night beside the lake, she was one of the most beautiful and enchanting creatures I had ever seen.

In Irish legend the warrior Oisín once hunted a hare and wounded it in the leg, forcing her to hide in the undergrowth. When Oisín followed he found a door leading underground. Eventually he emerged into a palace where he found a beautiful young woman sitting on a throne, bleeding from a wound in her leg.

As I learned to live in the silence of this new place, I would continue to encounter hares from time to time. Sometimes one would gallop past me in the lower meadow, long legs stretched out to full capacity, like a furry sprite whizzing past. Once at a secure distance, they would come to a halt and stare back at me. These large, well-muscled, arresting animals have never ceased to fascinate.

Then for some reason, a female decided to leave her newborn leveret behind a flower pot up against the wall of the house. The following year she left a set of twins in the very same spot. She returned occasionally to feed the young, but for the most part they were left to grow and survive on their own as is usual for hares.

Leverets are furry bundles, small and vulnerable. Unlike rabbits who dash in and out of their burrows to stay safe, hares lounge around in long grass and make nests there to sleep and relax during the day. Perhaps the hares were leaving their young close to our house because it felt safe from predators. Or maybe the land that they had once thrived on, had been so overrun by hunters that there was nowhere else.

During these early years in our new home the hare families spent many hours sunning themselves in the wild garden, or snoozing on the patio outside my office window. I was close enough at times to study closely their twitchy noses and enormous back legs and feet. They grazed fussily on my herbs and sat in the flower beds chewing on petals. After eating, they would sit with faces turned to the sun, or do their yoga, stretching out their long limbs, scrunching up their noses and grooming their ears.

I began to associate the hares with a kind of meditation. Sometimes they would simply sit still and stare into space for a long time. Their long ears might move with the slightest whisper of wind. But often they would close their eyes and appear to zone out.

The hare is a universal symbol of fertility and growth. Years later in the shop windows of Berlin, I saw the Easter Hare surrounded by chocolate eggs. This connection between the hare and fertility is still very much alive and well all over Europe.

Sadly the reclamation of land here in more recent years has reduced the habitat for wild hares and I didn't see any around here for a few years. But then recently my son spotted a leveret and its mother in the undergrowth behind the house. Later, in the moonlight I caught her shadowy figure and enormous bright eyes on a trail camera. She was heading away out the gate, perhaps leaving the leveret hidden somewhere in the long grass.

A month or so passed until my son again caught sight of not one but two young leverets behind the house. In no time they were grazing at the back door and snoozing in the sun

in the garden. Once more I had the privilege of watching hares grow up. Within six months they were both enormous! You wouldn't believe how their picky grazing could lead to such fine physique.

Messy and all as it appears, our garden of undergrowth and vegetation gone wild, with its brambles, ferns, long grass, self-seeded willows or gorse, allows a few of these animals to recreate a slice of habitat that is often lost in the monoculture of modern farmland.

BIRDS

Over time we settled into our new home and were mesmerised by the animals, birds and butterflies that lived alongside us. Eventually I learned to feed the birds every day throughout the year and not just in spring. Feeding them consistently has allowed a diverse population of birds to thrive here. I bore everyone by encouraging them to start a routine of feeding birds so that they become your friends. Not in a sense that you will be taming wild birds, but so that their presence will fill your life with song, chattering, fluttering, arguing amongst themselves and producing offspring.

Birds will tell you that spring is here even if you haven't noticed. I listen out for their conversations and music, following them with my lens. The finches chat in groups on the willow branches, while starlings whistle and call to each other on the roof. The thrush chooses the highest gorse bush for her evensong, and the tiny robin perches as close as possible to my spot, almost talking back to me as I chat to him. When the sparrowhawk or the buzzard are nearby alarm calls can be heard as courageous little birds try to chase them away from their territories. The constant presence of birds soothes the soul.

We had no idea that pheasants, mainly bred in captivity by the local gun club, would be so tame. In spring the day starts here with a pair of them waltzing up and down at the kitchen door. The cock rises early, especially when he is puffed up and frantic about warning off competitors. The males parade their exotic colours, striking up arguments with their own reflections in our window panes.

There is of course a family dynasty here now who have-managed to survive the annual shoot. You can tell them from the rest as they have no human-imposed tags on their legs and continue to breed in the wild garden.

The hen, on the other hand, is always nervous and, although she needs the food, keeps a low profile except to eat. They nest on the ground, building a well-protected grassy circle with six or seven eggs hidden in the undergrowth.

Later, pheasant chicks will accompany her on the lane

having a leisurely stroll. At first, we often see her with three, then two and finally one remains. The cock has long gone and the little family takes their chances on the farmland beyond.

There are also other feathered couples working in harmony to build their nests and raise the next generation. One year a pair of goldfinches built one just outside the kitchen window, hidden amongst the dark green leaves of a bay tree. As the young hatched out, there was intense feeding, and the parents would be over and back across the window, morning noon and night. When the time came I witnessed all five fledglings emerge from the nest and join the adults in a nearby birch tree.

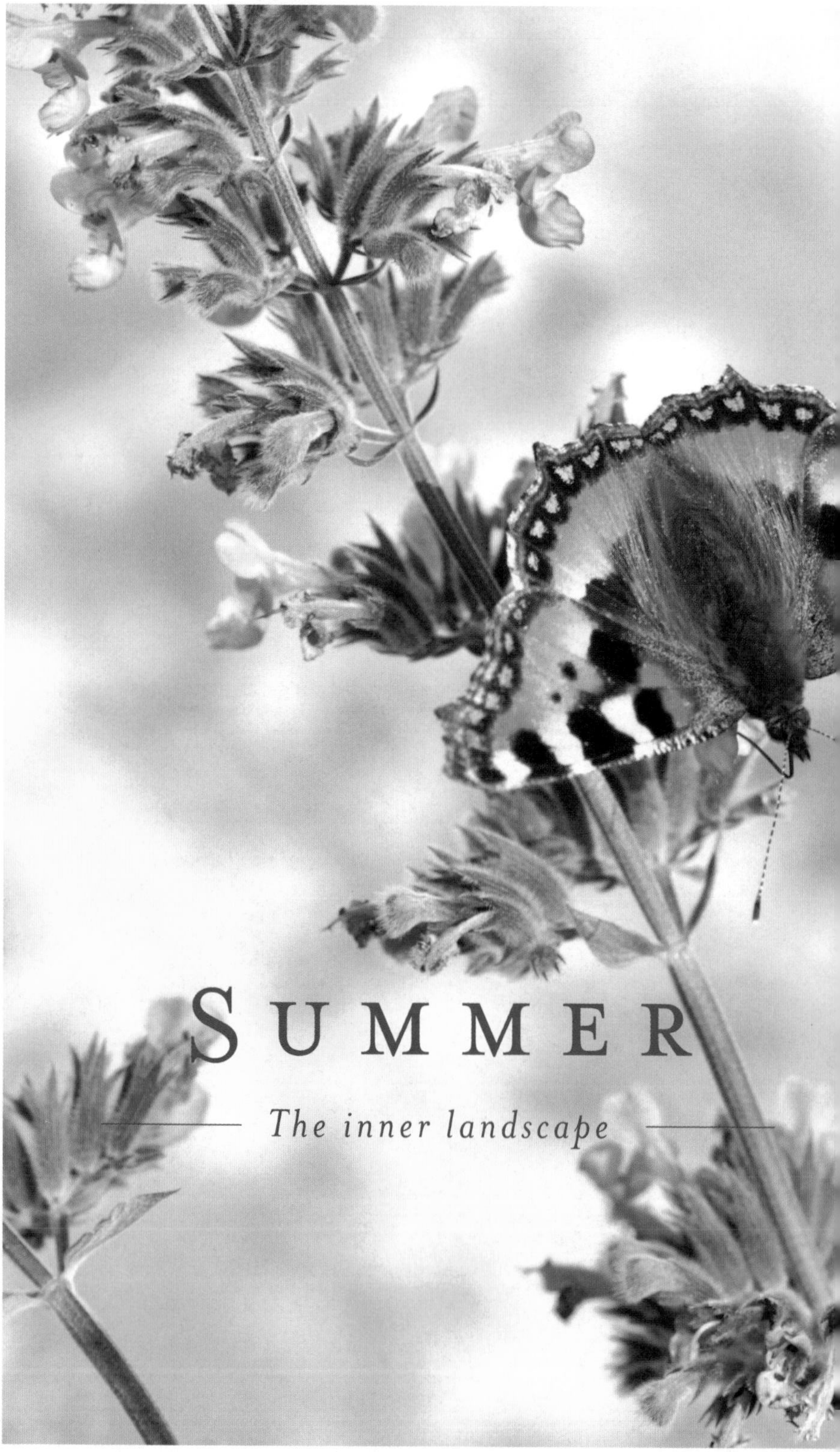

SUMMER

The inner landscape

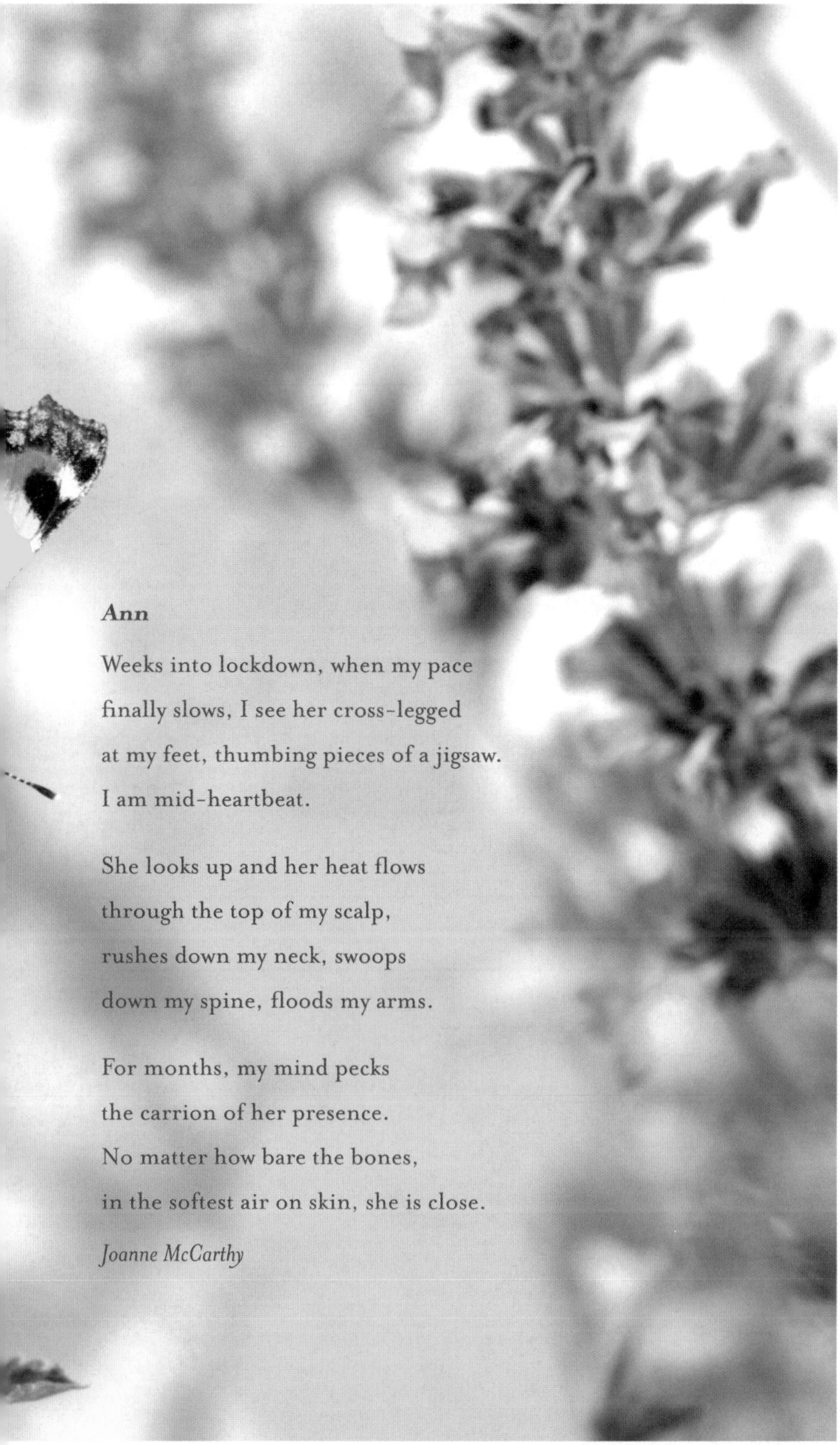

Ann

Weeks into lockdown, when my pace
finally slows, I see her cross-legged
at my feet, thumbing pieces of a jigsaw.
I am mid-heartbeat.

She looks up and her heat flows
through the top of my scalp,
rushes down my neck, swoops
down my spine, floods my arms.

For months, my mind pecks
the carrion of her presence.
No matter how bare the bones,
in the softest air on skin, she is close.

Joanne McCarthy

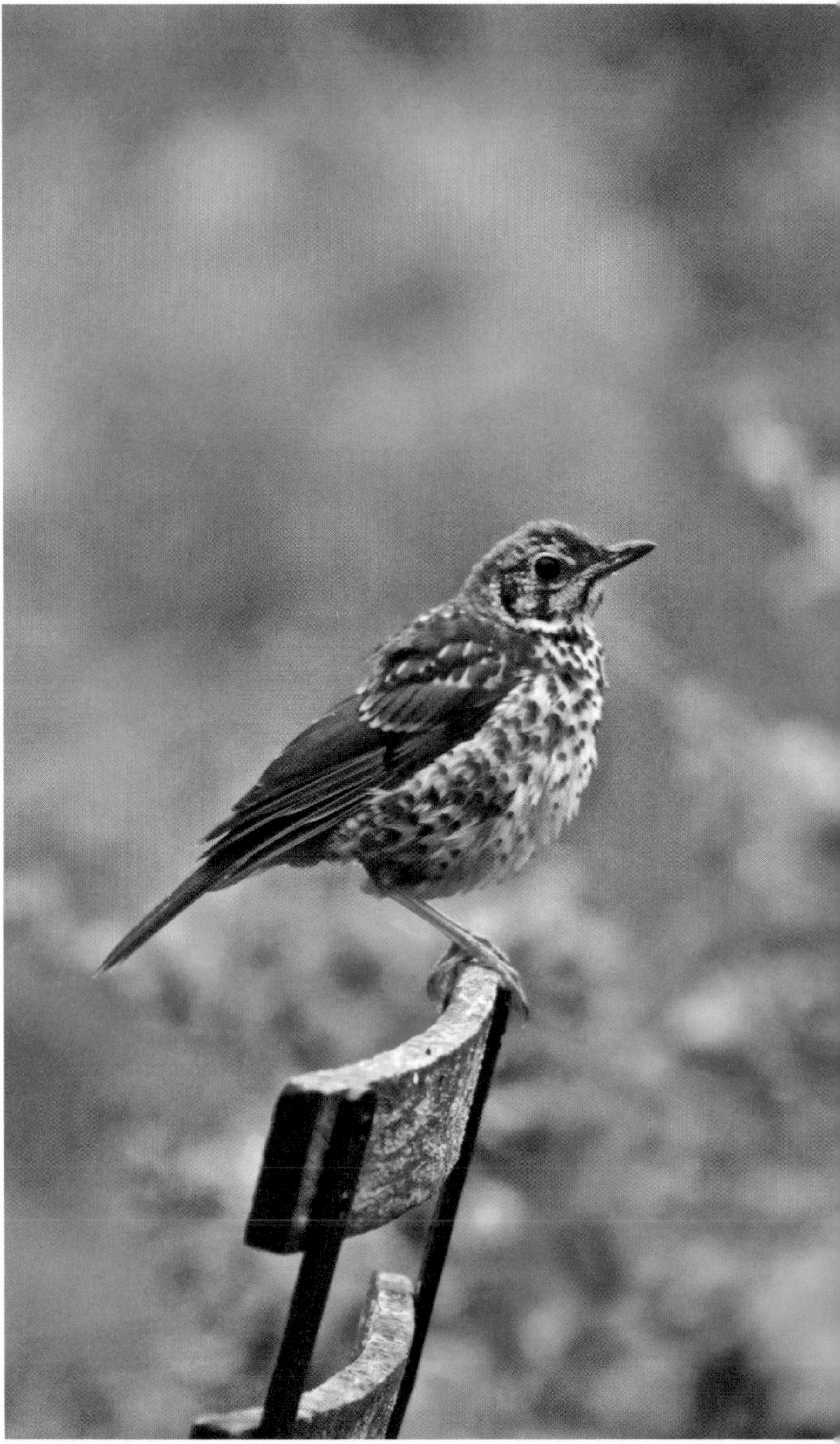

Chapter 5

The rose-petal path

IN THE FLOW

Flow, or being in the zone, is that creative space where you are oblivious to time. Children, once they are in the flow state, won't be aware of who you are or what you are saying while they are lost in that favourite activity or game. Anyone who is doing the thing they love and the thing they are good at knows this flow state well. Flow is also a state of solace for me.

Watching people who are in the flow is contagiously relaxing. They are like large ruminators, chewing the cud. Today, I am observing my Right-Hand Man as he builds a stone wall. He is fully engrossed; hours pass and I can see he is staring at a rock or even a small stone, for ages, completely lost in the activity of wondering where it will fit; which way up or down, beside which colour, or in which particular open spot. One of my neighbours used to express this kind

of labour as 'no strain' as he dug and heaped soil onto his perfect potato drills.

I have always taken photographs since I was given a camera for my tenth birthday. While I was an art student I struggled with the huge cost of equipment and printing. Now with digital photography there is new found freedom to photograph everything and anything around me. The camera adds another dimension to looking and seeing. Observing nature through the magic of a camera lens allows all of the extraordinary living detail to be revealed in full.

Solo walking with the camera opens up this creative flow space. The combination of eye, lens, frame and closure of the shutter brings about a kind of time outside of time. There can be no distraction as the lens literally focuses the mind on one thing only. With this practice, the pace of my daily walking slowed even more to the point that it was no longer even exercise. There was no compunction at all to stride out. Standing still would be a more accurate description of most of it!

MEMORY

Along these walks random sights, sounds and scents could trigger snapshot memories from childhood: the startling puce colour of foxgloves and how we used to put the trumpet-shaped flowers on our fingers; seeing the hairy legs, bulging eyes and veined wings of bees; the sweet scent of bluebells on the forest floor.

Most of all I began to remember preschool life with my mother, just the two of us together during the long day in a two-up two-down red-brick terraced house close to the border with Northern Ireland. I was Addie's firstborn daughter of four. I don't know if we called her Mammy or Mum, to us she will always be the girl who was our mother for a short while, and we call her Addie.

I lived with her until I was nine, but I only have slight and dreamy images: Addie playing her piano, in the kitchen making a steak and kidney pie, pushing a pram through the town to get to the music shop, the constant piano playing that was her release, her creativity, her solace.

If Addie's flow was in music, at that time, mine was in a box full of scented rose petals and honeysuckle that for days I collected in the small back garden. All summer long,

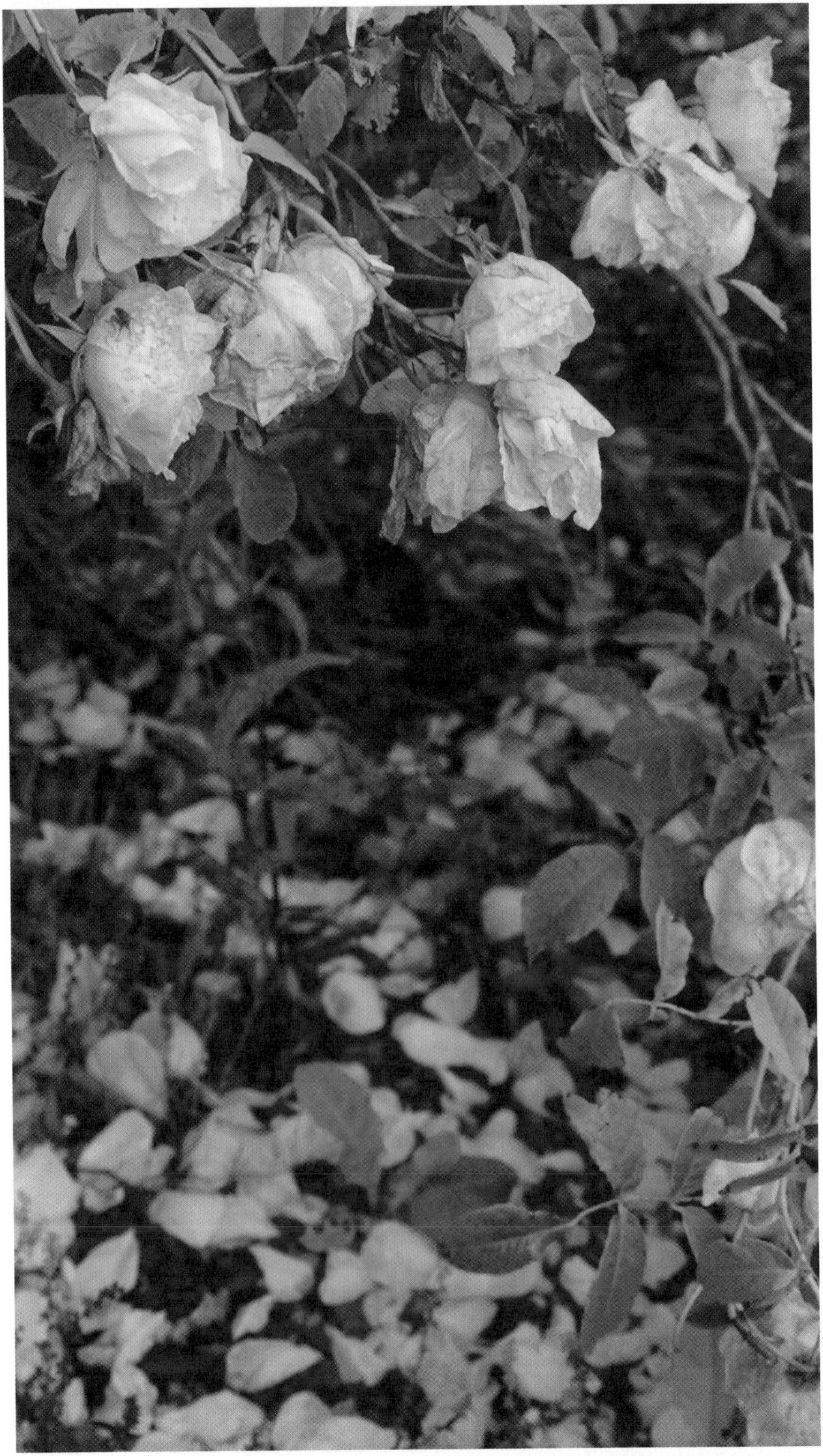

every morning along the path, there was a new crop of fallen flowers. Indoors and out of doors Addie and I were each engrossed in our own worlds.

From being with Addie while she played, I absorbed how to be in this state of flow, a kind of zoning out while zoning in. I used to wonder if Addie was feeling sad and would pause and listen to the emotive playing that brought tears to my eyes. She was very far away from her home and family in the midlands, where she had lived in a bustling market square. I've no doubt she was missing her previous life and was very alone in her married life in a northern town, where my father had been newly posted.

It wasn't just raw emotion, though, it was also that Addie had gone into that place of blissful attentiveness that we all find in the flow of creativity. Her playing was all consuming and while I sat on the stairs with my copybook and crayons, or wandered about in the small garden, I felt intensely a part of the mood.

These early memories of beautiful, dark-haired Addie, who was living her last few years, came fully alive to me in the mysterious bliss of flow in my rural ramblings. The beauty of the natural world around me somehow had re-established an almost physical connection to her. There was a oneness between Addie, me and Mother Earth.

ROSE PETALS AND HONEYSUCKLE

Even in that small back garden there was an abundance of nature – an exciting world outside the back door, overgrown

and stretching out to where I would play, make and hum.

There was a shed and a kennel for the dog Timmy in the yard. We would ignore each other as a rule. Passing by I would toss him a few words or give him a wide berth and wander further up the path. Timmy didn't last too long as my dad said he was vicious and he went to 'live on a farm' as was the custom.

The garden with the wonky path down one side and an unruly grassy patch on the other had roses tumbling down in heavenly bouquets and tiny creatures roaming the verges. I was drawn to beautiful scents and conjured up many watery concoctions of roses, honeysuckle and bluebells.

These days I don't see snails in the vast quantities that I saw them as a child, maybe due to a different balance in the garden habitat. Each one had a unique spiral shell, a tiny face with horns on its head, and slithery emissions that left glistening trails along the path. I traced my fingers along their shells and tried to coax their funny faces out by chatting to them. I gathered these cooperative companions up again and again, conducting them in my choir or lining them up for classroom lessons.

In that back-garden world there were the sounds of other families filtering through the fences on either side. On the boundary with our neighbour on one side was a hawthorn tree, old and gnarled, laden with rags and wishes. These could be prayers for an ill relative or scraps of paper with what was called an 'intention' written on it. A faery tree, it had a forbidden air about it. I would squint at it from a distance and sometimes be bold enough to stand under it, looking up into the blossom. But it was a no-go area and

even the adults held it in high esteem.

I collected conker shells and filled them with golden dandelions to make beds for my faery folk friends. Sometimes I buried a treasure, hoping that they would find it, returning over and over again to see if the treasure was still there.

Rose petals and honeysuckle were so abundant that I kept them in my pockets or made them into ladies' perfume or desserts for my doll. When I discovered mint, I made stews of stones, clay, water and bunches of mint leaves, stirring the mixture dreamily. I was a girl with an outdoor kitchen cooking up dishes with gusto.

INNER WORLDS

Sometimes when I close my eyes I can still see Addie, head bowed, her hands waiting on the piano keys. Hardly breathing, I am absorbing the moment with her, feeling with the music, and staring into a shaft of light coming through the window onto the busy street. I am often just waiting for the profound impact of her music.

Addie and I were relaxed companions, each in our creative flow. Her gift to me was sharing this: the importance of a rich inner world, a safe space to be in the moment, without fear or judgement. Over time, and despite how long it took, I have continued to learn how to cultivate this space and find solace in making.

Addie was the youngest child in her family of four. Her extraordinary parents, both creative and rooted in their midland communities, made a good life for their family at that time. Running two businesses — a restaurant for her and a cabinet-making workshop for him. I only now realise that they were prosperous by the standards of the day.

The story goes that Addie was a wilful child, sticking her tongue out at restaurant patrons who she took a dislike to. As a teenager she became organist in the local church and conductor of the choir.

Years later, I was given a letter she wrote to her aunt, a nun 'on the missions', where she declared her desire to become a nun and to avoid at all costs the typing course that her mother, my Nanan wanted her to join.

I remember being a teenager myself and writing to a charity in Africa asking about coming out there to do mission work. I pretended I was a man and they responded, but addressed the letter to Mr Drea. Of course my father opened it and had a fit that I was even considering going so

far away. I never knew until last year that Addie and I had something like that in common.

Addie's home place in the market square of a midlands town was abuzz with activity. The rambling building where she grew up had once been an RIC (Royal Irish Constabulary, the police force of the time) barracks. When Addie lived there it had a restaurant downstairs, a cabinet makers outside in a workshop and living quarters upstairs. While the adults managed their work and the numerous grandchildren, we were sent to this backyard to play.

The yard was a place of magic for us. It still had an isolation cell for prisoners converted into the men's toilet. At the end of the yard were two huge sheds full of furniture and best of all the local cinema adjoined the side wall.

Many evenings were spent listening to the latest film booming out of this cinema while we sat on the rockery playing with our dolls and teddies. Our favourite was anything

spooky by Alfred Hitchcock and when we were really lucky Nanan would send us down to Mr Bunny who ran the cinema where we would actually sit inside to see the film on the big screen.

Addie grew up here, and benefited from the family's prosperity after the Second World War. Her wedding to my dad looked to be large and glamorous and amongst the gifts was a rose tea set of which a few pieces remain today. She must have looked forward to her new life, a family and a long and happy future. Sadly this was not to be.

What's a hippopotamus?

When the house was full of that raucous music, I sat on the bottom step of the stairs. The next step up was my pretend grown-up school desk. School was my dream. In school I

would write and read and make friends. I practised every day for school.

I loved more than anything my new, blank, orange copybook. It had rows of thick red lines with thin blue lines in between. On each set of lines a large squiggle indicated the letters of the alphabet. I learned to copy each one and make proper writing.

I used to sit and wait for the playing to end. At the end of this hall was the door to the world. I watched the sun shining down out there on the street. Shadows would flicker across the mat. The mat where the letters fell like precious gold. Letters from home that made Addie happy.

A shaft of sunlight would creep up the hall during the day. I would be very absorbed in doing my sums. I could do three rows of numbers and a big plus sign. But all I wanted was to go to school. Proper school and learn more about sums. Who knew that I would turn out to be pathetically bad at maths all through my school life! In the background Addie's voice would fill the house. She would run through the repertoire: *Oft in the Stilly Night*, *Believe Me If All Those Endearing Young Charms*, *The Last Rose of Summer*.

As the morning passed, the sun would stretch up the hallway and reach my toes. I would dip my sun-soaked feet in and out of a shaft of warm sunlight, relaxing in the heat. I would stretch both my legs along the bottom steps of the wooden stairs. And then the sun crept up my whole body, until I put down my play copybook and lay there. Listening with closed eyes.

Sometimes she called for me. Because it was time to learn a new song. I used to stand beside the piano as she opened the big hard book with black scribbles or maybe a small paper book with writing and more scribbles. We collected these little books of music every week from a shop down the town. 'Ah,' the man would say, 'Mrs Drea, I have it here all the way from Dublin.' She would take the new music book in her two hands. They would talk some more. Then she asked for something new — something about a 'hippopotamus'. The man wrote it down.

'I'd say that will be next week at the earliest. Drop in on your way by.' There was no 'on your way by'. We only ever had one destination — this shop, with all its little books and records. This shop every week for a new music book that she would pore over all day. And now this shop would soon have a hippopotamus.

Later, the fire would be lit and she would make dinner. Ham with cabbage and potatoes, followed by apple tart, made with a long rolling-out of pastry in the tiny back kitchen. Or maybe mushroom omelette, which she said was very exotic. A small light would glow golden from the radio. Addie would hum along to all the tunes. And when I joined in she was delighted.

I can also remember being left with a swirling question, 'What is a hippopotamus?'

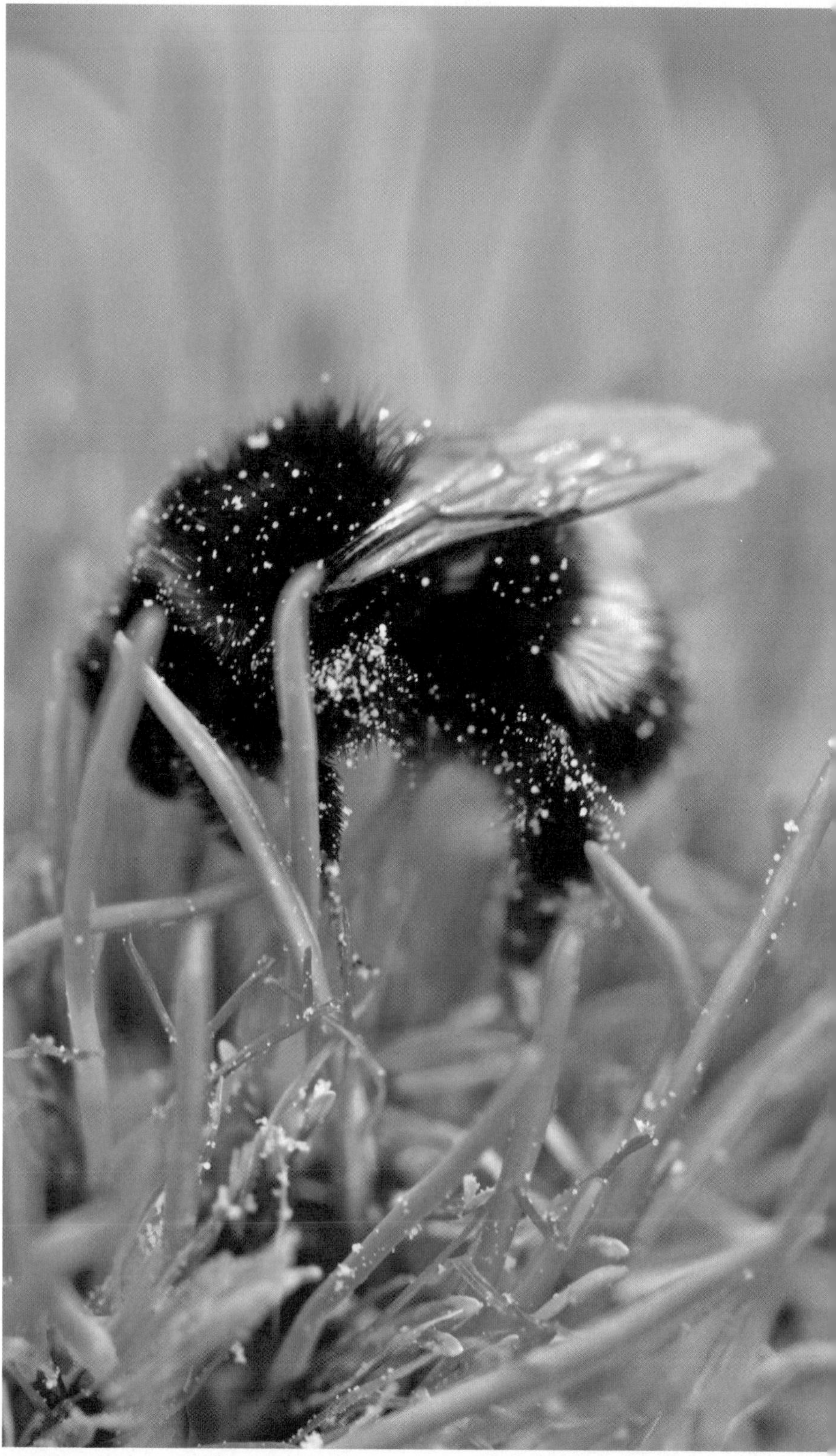

THERE'S NO PLACE LIKE HOME

During these years, alone in the small back garden, life was quiet and predictable. That little two-up two-down, red-brick house with the overgrown garden was our world. Myself and Addie were in peaceful harmony. I felt free and independent and Addie was happy with her music or with one of the new baby sisters in the house.

We practised singing the 'Hippopotamus Song' (Flanders and Swann, 1960) together, and I studied the drawings on the cover of the sheet music. We loved the way the hippo sang to his hippo girlfriend of the 'mud, mud, glorious mud' – 'nothing quite like it for cooling the blood'.

From then on, our world expanded at an alarming rate. In the next few years we would be challenged way beyond what any of us were expecting. So, like Dorothy in the *Wizard of Oz*, all through my growing-up years, I just wanted to click my heels together in the ruby slippers and repeat the magic spell … there's no place like home, there's no place like home …

In reality, I was never able to go back to that time or that little house with the rose-petal path. But now at least I can remember it. The true solace of feeling at home.

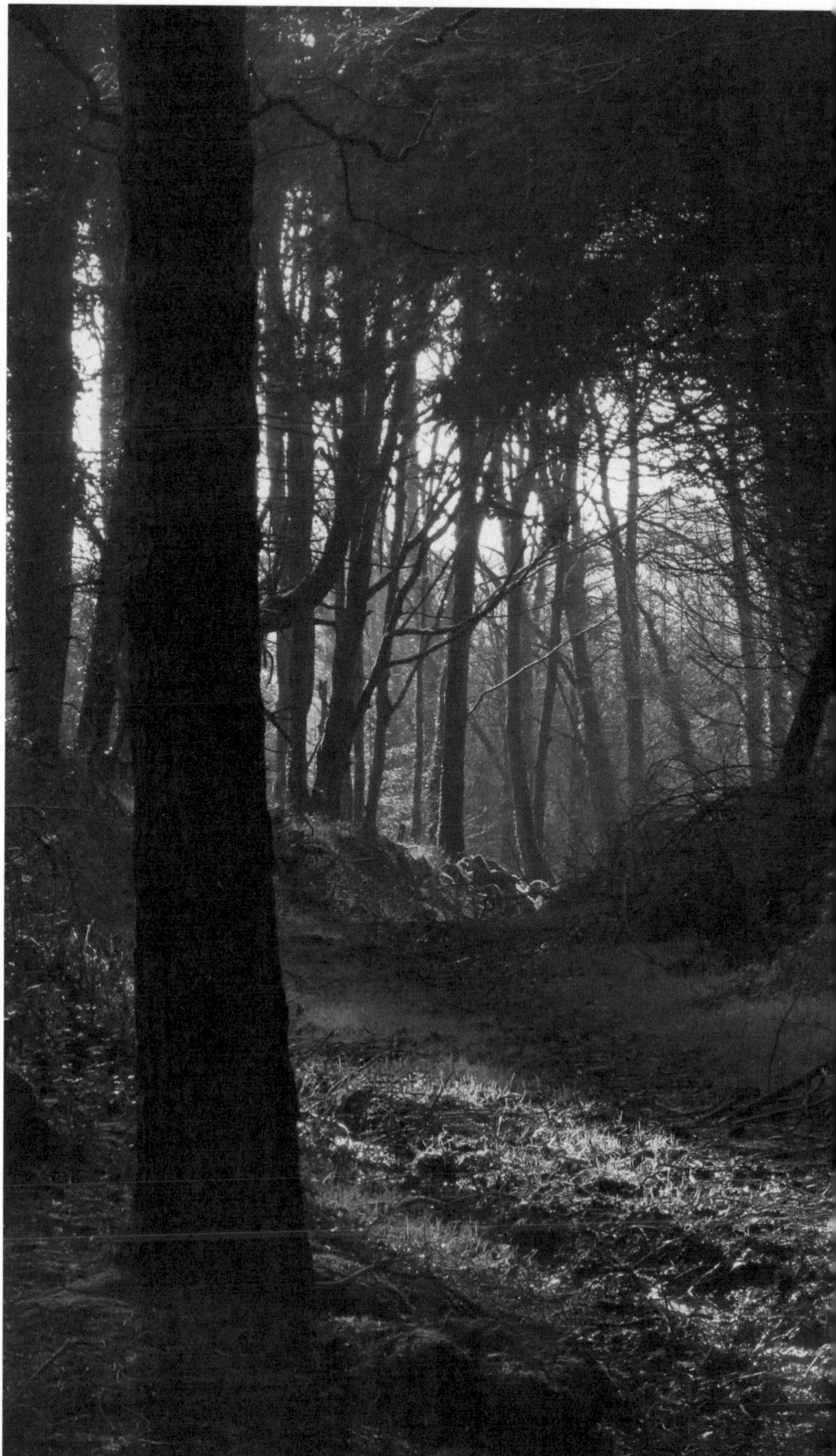

Chapter 6

An encounter with the wild

Awakening

Children can grow up starved of the natural world, and girls in particular are still often coached to stay clean and to beware of everything. There is so much to miss by the limitations of shrunken worlds. By the start of adolescence young girls have a roaming space about a third the size of boys, are generally terrified of moths and spiders and often don't even aspire to owning a pair of strong walking shoes.

Forests are magic, but there was always a certain anxiety about going 'down to the woods' when I was a girl. Deep, dark forests featured quite a lot in the stories and songs of childhood: 'Little Red Riding Hood', 'Robin Hood', 'Snow White' and the 'Teddy Bears' Picnic'.

You knew never to go anywhere alone. The first woods I had the chance to explore were close to the new house that my parents were building on the outskirts of the town. The small two-up two-down terrace with the wonky path would be no more. A bungalow on the Dublin Road was the 1960s house of my parents' dreams.

We began to visit the site as the house was built. For the first time myself, aged seven, and Grace, my sister, younger by three years, were kitted out in corduroy trousers and wellie boots. In these clothes we could run in and out of puddles and up and down mounds of builders' sand. The winter of 1962–1963 was one of the harshest of that century as the ponds froze and the temperatures plummeted.

I had been very resistant to Addie's image of what a girl should be and had hated dressing up in flouncy dresses and had detested the pipe cleaners used as hair curlers in particular. There's a photo of me at the time, my face a luminous moon, wide-eyed with straight hair, although Addie had made many efforts to fix it. Fancy dresses just never looked good on me, so there I am in a tartan skirt and woolly jumper.

The girl next door, pictured in the photo, has a pink sticky-out dress made of fine netting. She is a princess with raven-coloured hair and red lips. It's when I see her, in all her glory, that I realise I was never meant for frilly dresses, much and all as Addie would have wished it so. One day I found scissors on Addie's dressing table and cut a huge chunk out of my fringe. My first but not my last protest haircut!

In our new outfits of boots and trousers, Grace and I

hooked up with a gang of kids from the nearby estate who knew the ropes and that's when the next adventures began as we escaped to the surrounding fields and roads.

WANDERING

Wandering the fields with our little gang was where the natural world expanded and I began to drift away from the safety of life in the small garden. Foraging and meandering in the spooky woods whetted my appetite for the wonder of rambling. Our favourite spot was the darkest grove of trees where we would be hoping for a good fright.

Going in under the canopy blocked the light and sounds of civilisation. Flickering shadows made a faery tale of the forest as the sun filtered through the leaves. Mosses grew thick and hairy on the stone walls and the forest floor was deep in

old vegetation that stuck to our shoes. Here and there, white wood sorrel flowers winked up out of the darkness.

Ahead was a path with a bright tunnel at the end as the wood opened up again into a clearing. We were strolling towards that light and filling our pockets with blackberries that had already soaked big purple stains on my clothes. I was a million miles away in my dreaminess when I was startled by a lot of finger-pointing into the trees and a cry of RUN! I had just enough time to bravely sneak a look at what exactly we were running from. Up there in a tree was an owl sitting upright, exactly as I had seen so many times in a book. I'm sure it hooted as it flew away.

The game was to RUN, so I ran with the rest of the kids and as we emerged from the woods we howled laughing at the craic of it. The fun was being scared, and owls qualified as very scary on our scale.

Years later, a long-eared owl decided to take a nap in a tree here in our garden. At first I thought it was a cat. I discovered that the long-eared owl is literally called *ceann cait* (cat's head) in Irish, because when sleeping and puffed up you would swear it was feline. I couldn't take my eyes off this owl, and was riveted to the spot.

An owl snoozing in broad daylight got me very excited and I took a lot of photos all through the day. She must have been exhausted as she never budged. Then, after a couple of hours, she sat up wide awake, with that startled owl look on her face.

Her amber eyes opened wide and we stood there, face to

face, eyeballing each other in a still and precious moment. Two animals meeting and looking into each other's eyes. I treasure and remember each time it happens that I have a one-on-one encounter like this with an animal, or a human for that matter.

Carefully, I tried to take more photographs. My inner child was at last reassured that there is absolutely nothing frightening about encountering an owl. It was astonishing to be there to see it at all. Since that first time in the scary woods, I had only ever seen owls float around the house at dusk or in the headlights of the car at night.

I used to question if there was too much mouse and vole activity at the bird feeders. But now I understood that the owls are only here for the supper of voles that has become available over the years. Not only are we required to feed the

birds, but also the rodents and therefore also owls and other larger predators.

But still in my naive view it is hard to accept that everything in the natural world eats something else.

Everything has its place

Allowing nature to take its course here has been an education in the fragility and the harshness of the wilderness. One day a pheasant flying past the house, hit the window and died instantly. I suppose a true country woman would immediately pluck it and have it for dinner. My green-fingered French friend would! She has the right knowledge and skills when it comes to what to eat and how.

Without a clue of what else to do throughout the day I photographed the beautiful dead pheasant, admiring her soft feathers and the pinkish tinge around her neck. Within

an hour a brown rat had arrived and was feasting on her now-stiff corpse.

At the best of times rats are a challenge because they can carry disease and they are very brazen animals. You are never more than six feet from a rat, people say. I try to accept the rat population's rights to territory along with all the other animals, but sometimes it's not easy. In a previous cottage where we lived our neighbour had to set a rat trap in the house for us after a large one came into the bedroom and tried to steal one of my shoes while I was asleep. I woke up to the sound of dragging and found him waltzing across the floor, with a sparkly shoe in his jaws.

By the end of the day, the brown rat in my garden was still gorging on the pheasant using his two pink hands to feed himself. I photographed this meal with a long lens and it is the closest I will ever get to such a bloody scene. By morning there was nothing left but a pile of soft feathers.

My father always said not to worry about rats, that ours are only nice country rats, and I decided then that he had a point. Not for the first time, I swallowed my prejudice and allowed someone or something to 'live and let live'. Everything has its place in the scheme of things.

A HIDE

While working from home, both after the economic crash and during the pandemic, I was often cooped up in the house so I used the desk at the window to watch the wildlife

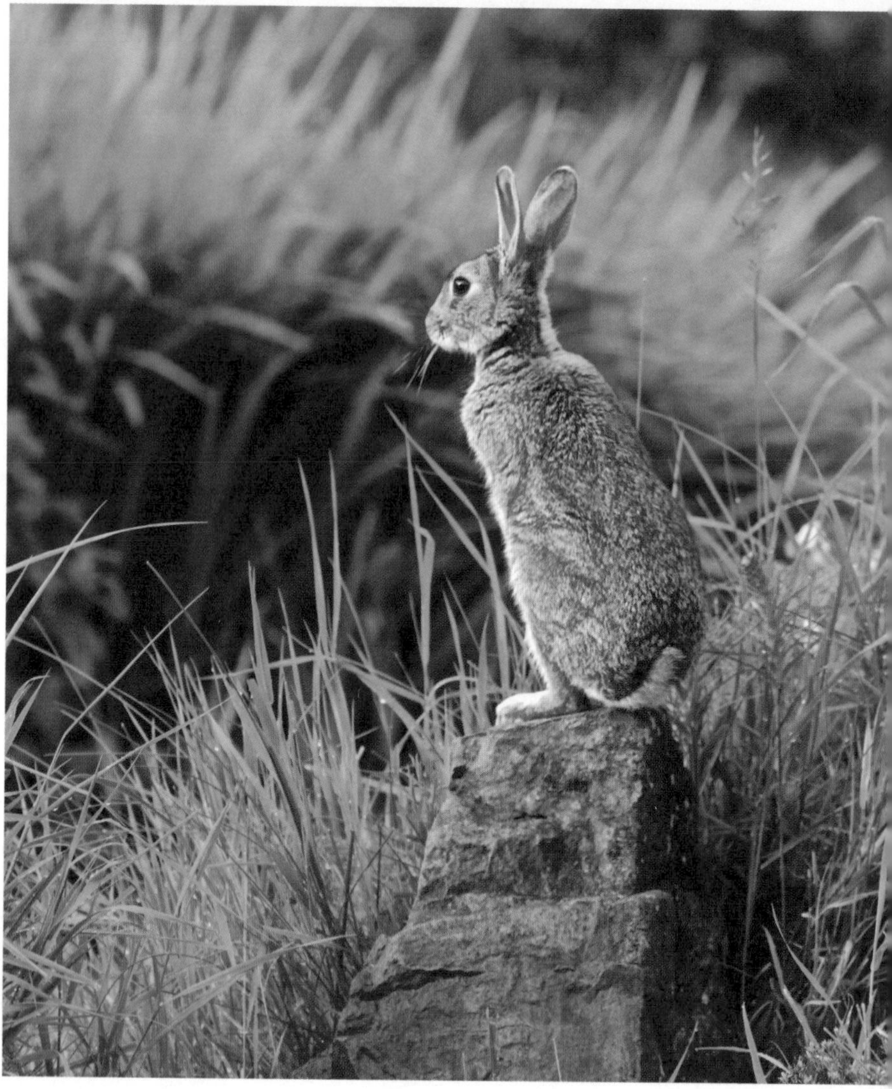

up close. It felt at times like my window on the world was a hide in some exotic location.

Besides all the usual daily events, every so often something spectacular would occur. So much so that I would be rooted to the spot, unable to reach for the camera. Even though I would miss the shot, my motto was that just being there was enough.

On one occasion my son came belting down the stairs saying that there was a stag running down the lower field. How or why we never fully figured out as there are few deer around here, but we both saw this beautiful animal, with a full head of antlers, go down to the lake to drink. Once, while talking to someone on the phone, a pine marten wandered up to the bird feeders, sniffed around and strutted on his way. Then there was the time with my youngest son that a fox crept past the window, stopped for a moment and stared in at us. It was lashing rain and the fox was dripping wet. We froze as he walked along examining everything and giving us an occasional dirty look.

Seeing these animals up close in the day time is rare enough unless they are in trouble like the young badger we once released from a trap. Rabbits and hares, my absolute favourites, are the exception to this and they don't seem to notice that we even live here at times. All close encounters with wild animals are balm for the soul.

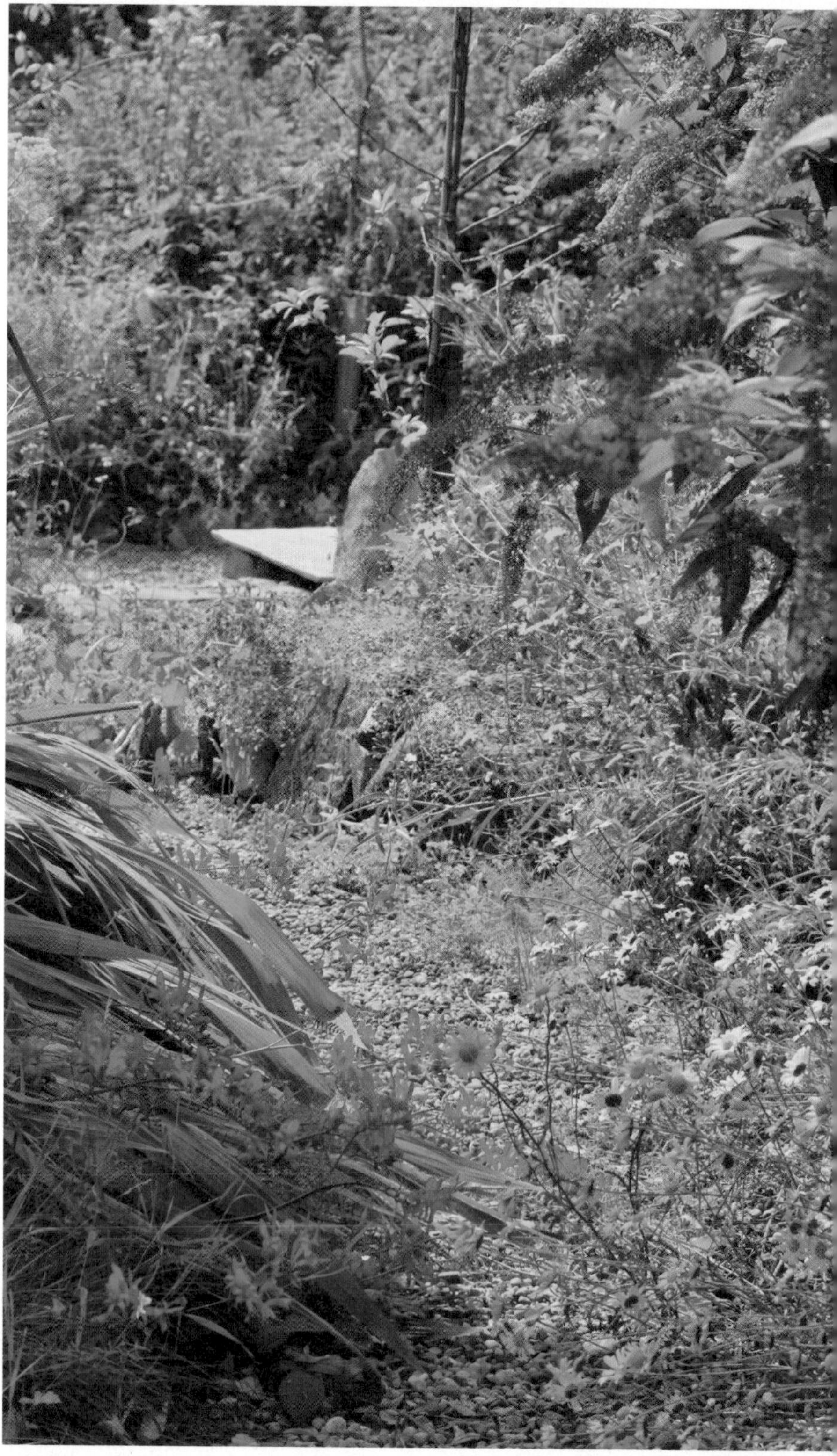

Chapter 7

Wild summer

PERFECTING IMPERFECTION

When the first true summer's day arrives, it comes with the softening of wind and a rise in temperature. The still air is full of the scent of blossoms and the beginnings of summer flowers. We shed our layers and enjoy the balmy slow walking in the warmth of the day, rare enough here on the edge of the island. There is a persistent weather flow coming up from the south west. On these days there is a shift to summer temperatures as warmer air moves up from France and Spain.

When it's hot, we drop everything. These precious days are for basking in the sun and for getting out the parasols to create some shade ... of all things! We eat outside, we sit and stare into the blue sky. Dragonflies, bees and butterflies give summer a first go. Is it really summer? We will all be hoping so, as the days continue to be settled.

My memories of scented flowers and the creepy-crawly undergrowth in that rose-petal garden of my early childhood probably inspired our wild garden of today. It is two and a half acres, although about half of it is a hill of rock, gorse and heather. Rewilding isn't so much about what you do, as what you stop doing. So the basics here are no mowing, allowing undergrowth to develop in its own way, with self-seeding and some planting of native species. The other rule is no dogs or cats so that wildlife can make a home here too.

It's not tidy! Someone once told me that this plot looks as if no one lives here and the whole place has gone to rack and ruin. In no time at all after you set about giving land back to nature, brambles will take over almost everything. Brambles are wonderful plants for bees and in the autumn produce juicy blackberries. I know this, but still I curse them when they so knowingly wrap themselves around my legs or trip me up as I scramble through to gather apples.

In this terrain of mainly acid soil the brambles then give way to ferns. Ferns will dominate most things too. Once they get a hold, they crowd out other species and spread rapidly. Ultimately over time, due to the self-seeding of a variety of trees that originally covered this wetland, a woodland is developing.

Trees seem to help everything come into balance. The brambles and ferns are marginalised and along with gorse are confined to the uplands and the rockier patches. Fast-growing willows attract birds and allow a lusher undergrowth of smaller plants to thrive in their shade. They flower and fruit profusely as they are happy in the boggy environment and so they self-perpetuate.

And the result is hope! Creating an oasis for wildlife and wildflowers in a sea of intensive farming, messy and all as it is, brings some optimism for the future of Ireland's shrinking biodiversity. From a barren grassland to a habitat for dozens of birds, hedgehogs, field mice and voles, insects, the Irish hare, and visiting foxes and badgers. And all around us the happy song of bees buzzing.

LUS NA MBAN SÍ

During the summer months, the mood is bright and light. The first foxgloves with their faery hats bloom in the undergrowth of trees and poke up in unexpected places. Bees are besotted too and creep up into the flowers, leaving nothing but their footprints inside. They grow in large drifts

along boundaries, in dappled shade, at the base of trees, and on cleared ground. The camera loves their translucent petals, their shapes and layers. The biennial foxglove once established, self-seeds and returns year after year. Without doubt, they are Ireland's most spectacular wild flower.

Some of their magic is in the glorious shades of cerise, the trumpet shapes of the flowers and their height often growing to three feet (around a metre) tall. They have a special magic and are associated with the myths and tales of faeries and wee folk. In Irish they are called *lus mór* (great herb), *méara cait* (cats' fingers), also *lus na mban sí* (herb of the faery women; this Irish name is also given to the white-flowered plant fairy flax) or *méirín púca* (little finger of the pooka), or *mearacháin táilliúra* (tailor's thimbles).

Underneath the foxgloves as they fade away, tall daisies grow. Selfheal unfurls beneath the daisies, and somewhere at the very bottom of this layered vegetation silky mosses cling. In the midst of these dreamy summer days, with the scent of meadowsweet in the air, the landscape is a tangle of lush green.

THE LAKESHORE

If you walk with me here in summer, we would have to take a wander down our lane to the lakeside. Here at the edge, between land and lake, we will be bathed in the scent of meadowsweet and wild mint underfoot. Dragonflies, butterflies and all the insects of the wetlands will flash and spin

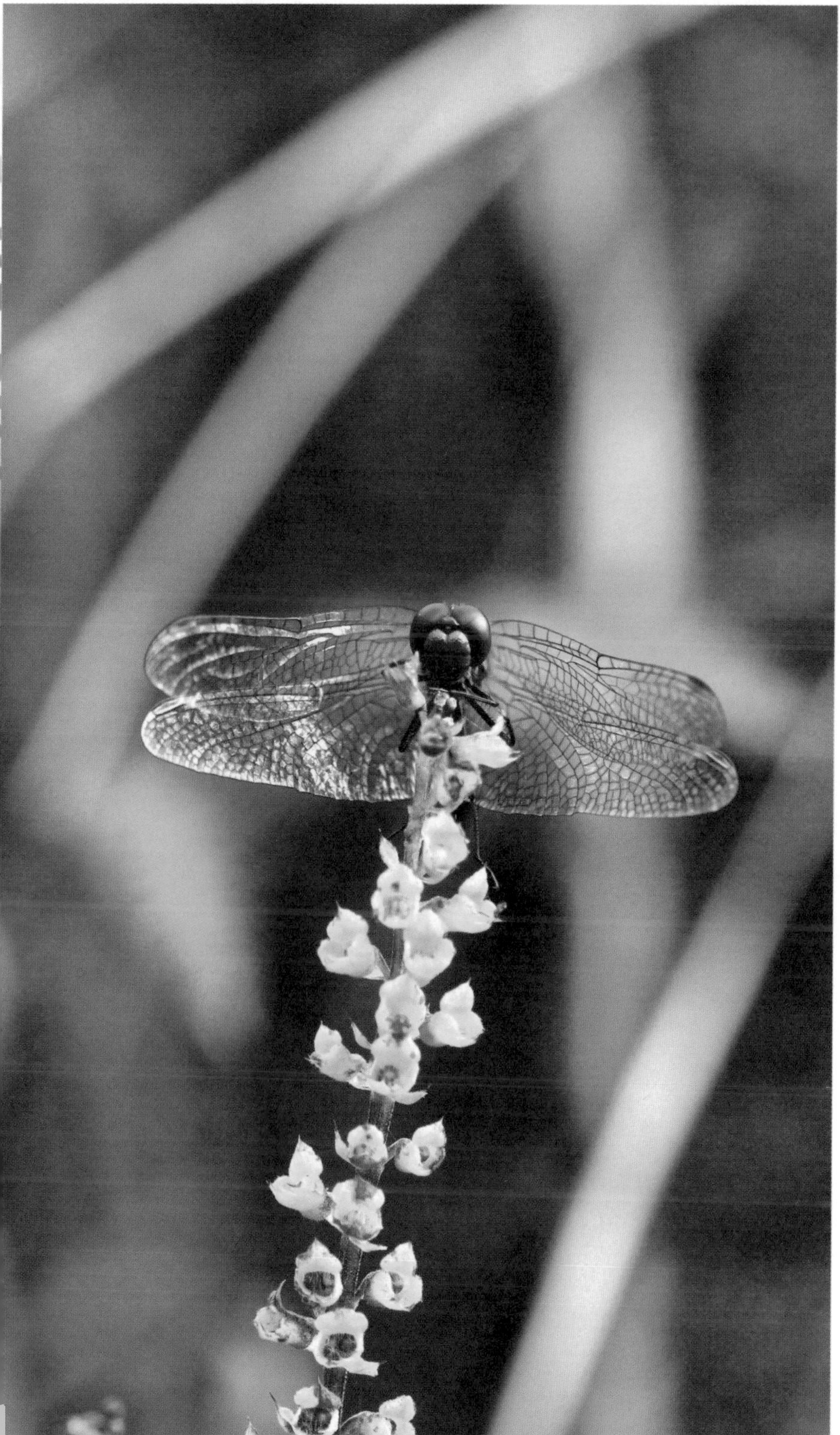

around the summer flowers.

We could even have a freshwater dip? The water is warm in summer. In the first few months after we moved here, my Swedish nephews were visiting. We were still building, had no running water and had not fully explored the area. The two lads, so familiar with lakelands, didn't think twice about wandering off down to the lake with wash bags under their arms, to jump right in.

For a moment or two you might feel hesitant about stepping into the unknown. We are not all familiar with deep still water. At my regular spot, you would first have to wade through tall reeds, a couple of metres overhead. Sometimes they spook me a bit, waving in front of my face or brushing against my legs and feet. Slowly pushing through a small tunnel made by summer swims, you eventually come to the open expanse of the lake.

The entire perimeter is lush and green. If you are used to the colours of the beach, then this swim is darker and deeper in tone. On calm days, the cool water eases out your shoulders and your whole body stretches to its fishy limits. Swallows accompany you dipping their beaks into the surface of the water as they fly by. Being out here is a deep inhalation of verdant summer.

Afterwards, as you find your way back to the meadow you step on wild mint and throw yourself onto the sun-warmed blanket. Here, dragonflies tease the photographer in me as I watch their wings glint with flashes of rainbow. The heron rises from its nest and a resident pair of swans drift by in the distance with their diminishing number of cygnets.

That mint-scented shoreline and the deep freshwater bring a peaceful heaviness and relaxation to the body, unlike swimming at the seashore, which is so invigorating.

Being immersed in water

Summer rambles are dusty and dappled. If we meet humans along the way, they will be chatting a few notches up the happy scale. Summer brings on exuberance like no other season. There is more to see, smell and feel on the surface of

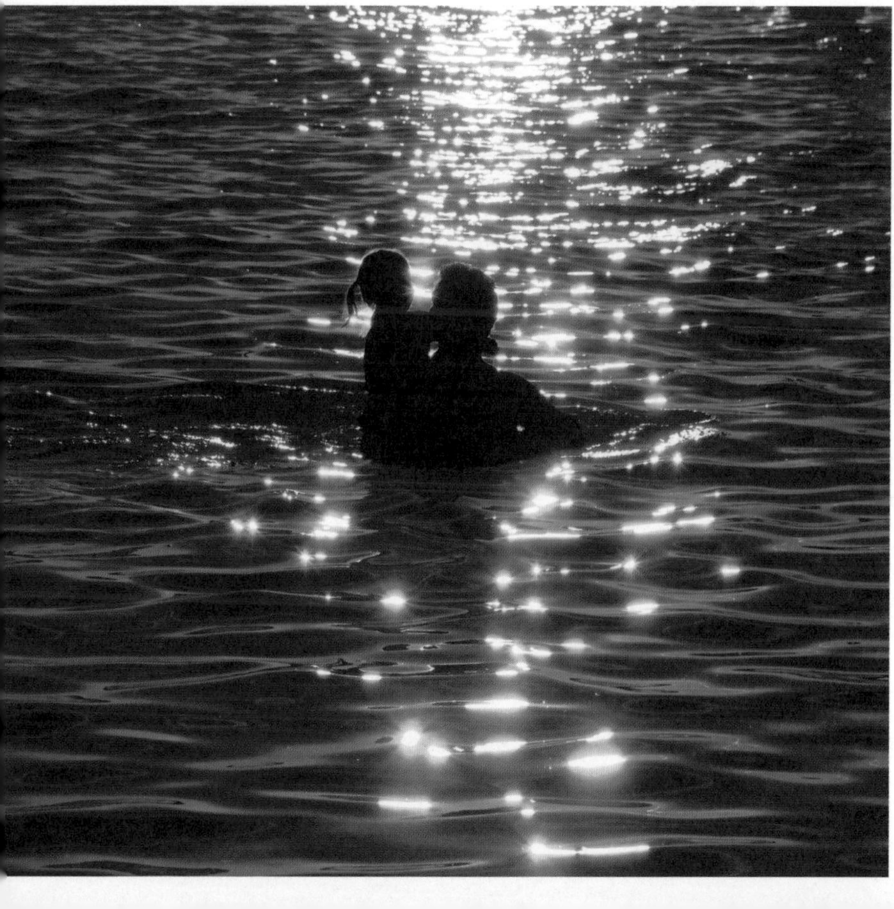

a summer walk; the light is sharper and sparklier.

At the farthest end of this walking trail, the path joins a country road. Because it is summer we should take this road as it eventually leads to the nearby seaside town of Tramore. Here the beach, especially at low tide, stretches for miles and opens up the land to the sky for as far as you can see. Birdwatchers explore the Back Strand, a haven for migrating birds. For others, the Sunday stroll on the Prom or the essential fish and chips at the Slip are the epitome of an Irish seaside experience.

Swimming at one of the many beaches along the Copper Coast is the height of summer pleasure. I treasure memories of sunny days on Annestown Beach, with a small baby under a canopy and a couple of naked toddlers running in and out of pools or being buried in the golden sand. On rainy days a deep sea swim in our own Boat Strand is a mesmerising experience, with raindrops creating patterns on the surface and the illusion that the water is warmer when the body is already wet getting in.

The best swims of summer remain with me too. Slipping into the harbour at Brandon Creek in Kerry, where St Brendan the navigator set off across the Atlantic to find America. Swimming there amongst the steep rocky cliffs; a silky and energetic swim shared with much-loved old friends, pulling sea spaghetti from the deep water to add to our fish dish of the evening. Or swimming in the River Nore in Kilkenny with my father, almost sixty years ago, feeling the novelty of freshwater, seeing him dive under like a big kid, and being able to swim with eyes open and not feel the salty sting of the sea.

The waters around the island of Ireland are cold at the best of times. I remember as a child being so cold in the sea that my teeth would be chattering. Dad would be standing on the beach shouting to come in and get dry. Arguments would ensue, with me insisting that I wasn't the tiniest bit cold, even when I couldn't feel my hands or feet.

Nothing heals the wilted like the sea. Nothing fills the mind with clear space like the cool Atlantic, in any weather. A sea swim always performs the same trick; whether its wind and waves further west, soft and balmy seas in the inlets, or swimming out to the rocks along the Copper Coast.

And then there is the best part, as the months flow on, the spirit of summer grows stronger and inhabits us. The land, the sea, the me. Part of it all. Breathing this world in. Breathing me out again. In a closer and closer bond. If the weather is great, every Irish person will say there is nowhere better to be on a summer's day. Although it can rain and be miserable, sometimes we are grateful too for a soft day that allows us to curl up, read a book and savour it all.

PRIMITIVE MAN

In summer young people roam the land here like lost tribes looking for a place to settle. Unused to these endless summer days, they take to building fires and gathering on the hills. As usual, like primitive humans before them, they leave their mark behind. Often the forest catches fire and yet again the hillside is blackened and charred.

They remind me of how 40,000 years ago, in a cave in El Castillo in the north of Spain, someone else lit a fire and decided to stencil her own hands onto the walls. Walking into that cave and seeing the resulting art, I instantly recognised that impulse. So I paint onto my own cave wall: watercolours, photo images, words, close encounters and all the space in between.

Summer always finds my inner child collecting random finds: pebbles, petals, twigs and old paints. Animal habitats

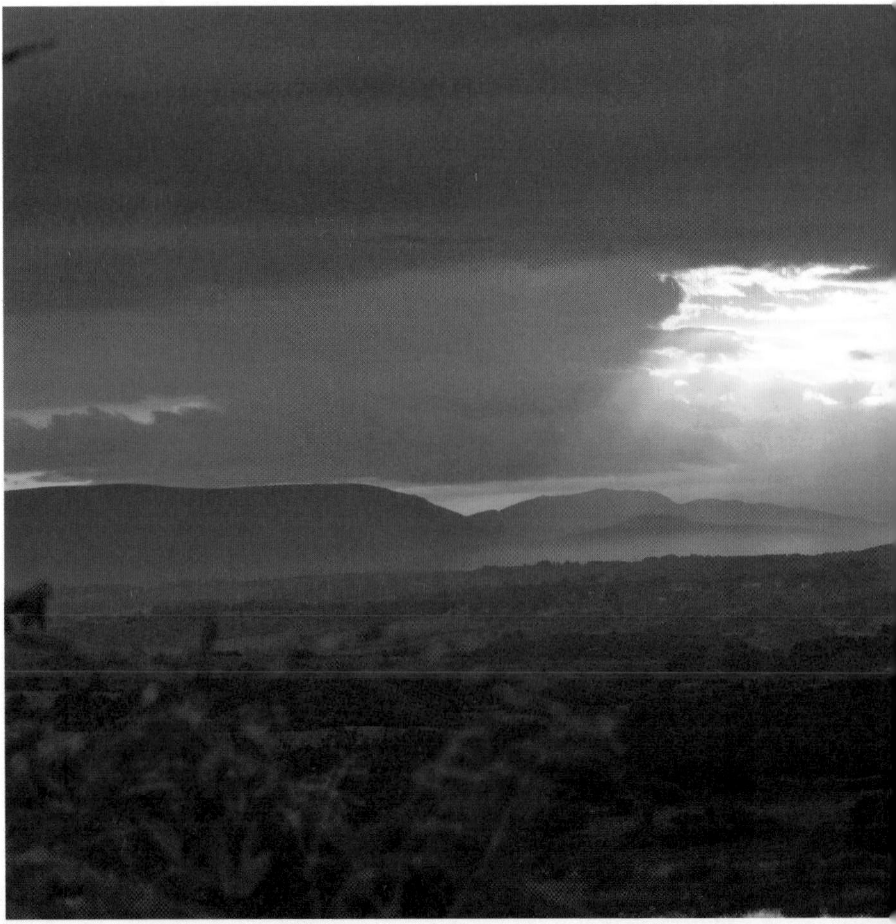

and my own are comfortably and harmoniously dancing in the summer breeze. We go about our creativity and survival with curiosity for each other, but a kind of oneness in our to-do lists. We breakfast together, we snooze in the sun, we meditate on life.

In the evenings the land turns towards the western sky and is warmly lit by the sun setting. Neighbours gather at the top of the hill overlooking the west of the county. 'You wouldn't get the likes of it in Killarney,' one says, gazing out over the wide valley, nothing between us and the foot of the Comeraghs. We are awed into silence as the sun goes down.

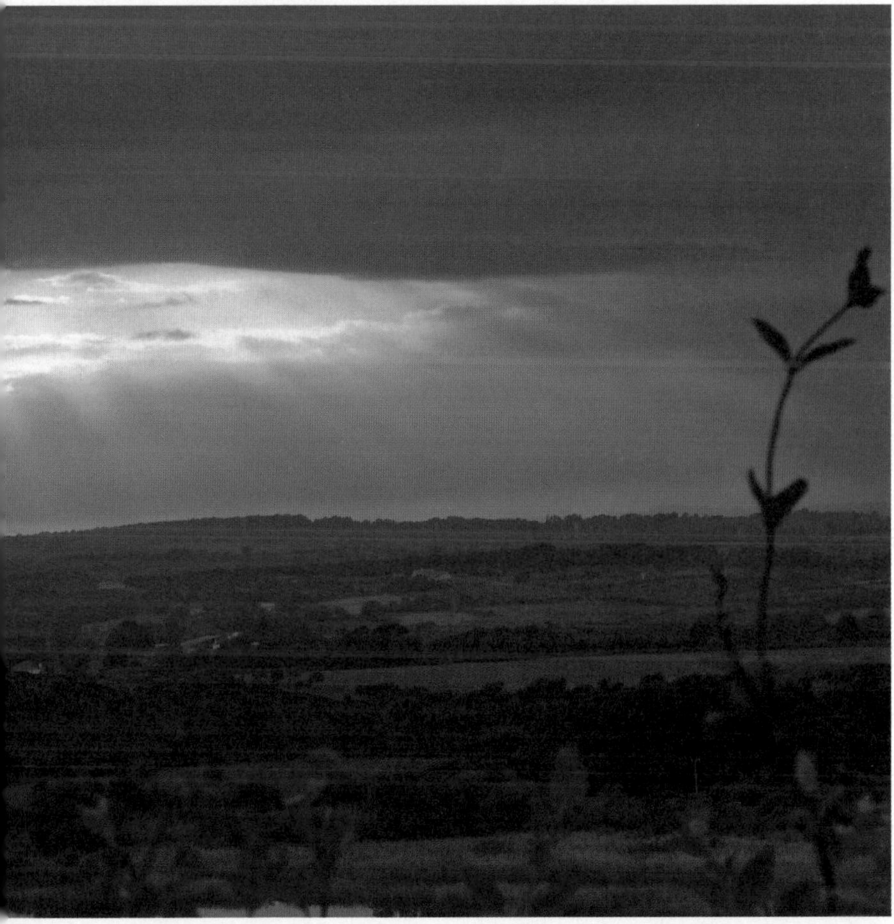

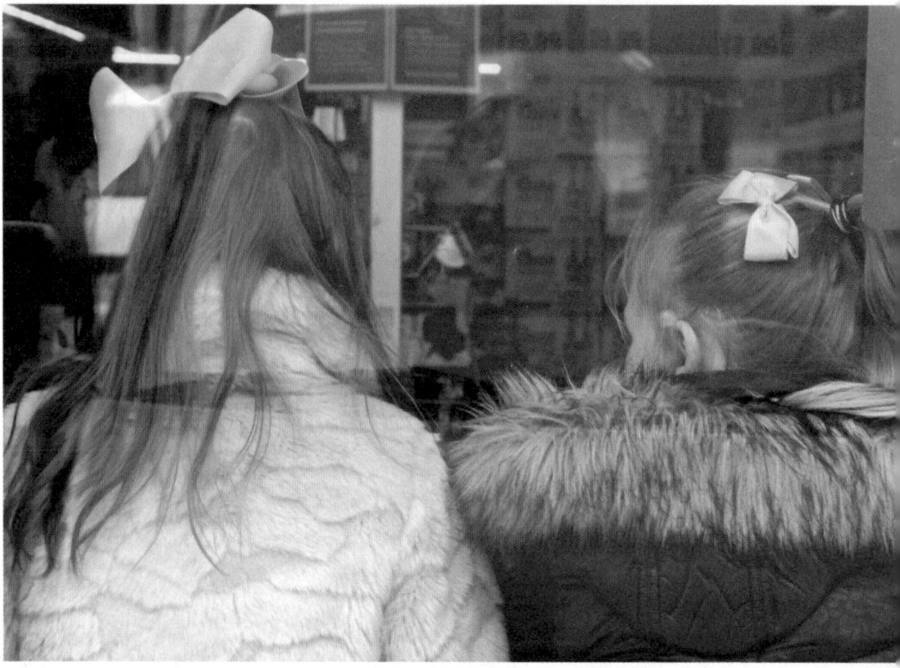

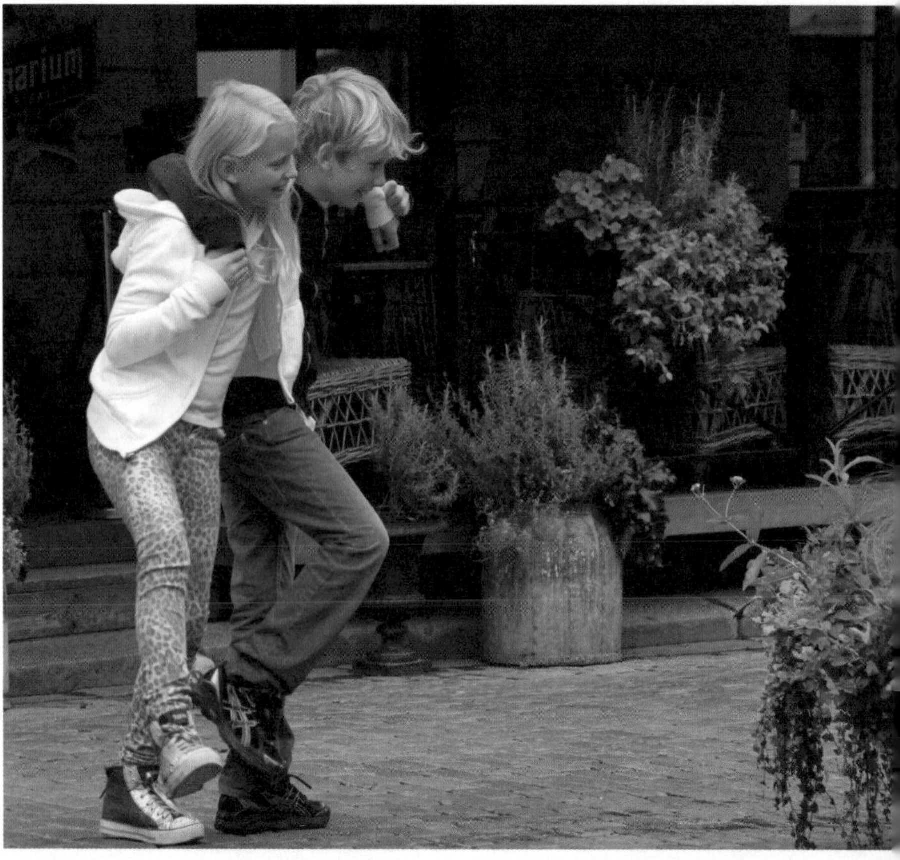

Chapter 8

Lost and found

Precious friendship

R elationships between children are often overlooked by adults. So many times I bonded with other children only to have to leave them behind as my parents moved on. They were my very first relationships outside of the family and the ones that shared fun and adventure. Every time we moved, there was another little gang of them in their unique territory that we would never see again.

In the new bungalow on the Dublin Road, our first small house that I knew every inch of soon began to fade into the past. But just as my world began to open up with more freedom to roam in this newly built house with its fitted kitchen, pink wallpaper for the girls' rooms and coffee tables with side lamps, life as I knew it was turned upside down once again. My dad announced that he had been promoted to Head Office and that we were moving house again, this time to Dublin.

I loved my school, my new bedroom in the bungalow; I was happy filling copybooks with poems about Africa and deeply emotionally involved in any number of issues I was learning about from the nuns. I'm not sure now which came first, Dad's promotion to Dublin or Addie's illness. But it was around this time that she was diagnosed with cancer. I didn't understand any of it and all I could think about was that I was losing my familiar life and gang of friends. How would I possibly survive without them?

By this time we were four sisters in the family; younger sister Grace was three years younger, Mary two years younger again and Melanie the new baby. In between Addie spending weeks in hospital and the uncertainty of how we would fit into our new life there was a transition time when we were sent to stay with relatives and moved from school to school. First our cousins' national school in the midlands and then, a few months later, another school near Dad's new office in inner-city Dublin.

I was longing as usual to settle into a proper routine and make new friends. A few weeks here and then there, and exposure to some new and very scary nuns, made me anxious and I began to complain. I had been slapped with a stick for getting sweaty hand stains all over my sewing sample. This was an elderly woman rearing up on a child who was trying to deal with being alone and away from home at the time. No wonder I was trying so desperately to be 'good'.

1963

Now our family moved to Number 2 of a housing estate in Dublin, with builders still on site and wild meadows all around. There were herds of horses in the fields behind the houses and gangs of kids from neighbouring estates wandering around looking for craic.

In those days, once breakfast was over, kids were shown the door. Addie by now was spending more time in hospital or in bed upstairs. As the summer went on, we saw less and less of her. Aunties and 'girls from the country' stayed over to look after us.

Our new back garden was still a pile of rubble so we would ramble out onto the unfinished roads. Next door in

Number 1 was a family of boys in Aran jumpers. They kept to themselves and we never got to know them. On the other side in Number 3 was what used to be called 'an only child', but she wasn't let out so we never got to know her either. The main interest in the area was a family of six children who lived in an old cottage with a vegetable garden and a chubby baby.

I first met them wheeling the baby out for a walk in a big old pram. The eldest boy, Sean, was the same age as me, eight going on nine. He was in charge of his siblings, as I was in my family. We hit it off straight away and so began our daily adventures.

The adults had absolutely no idea what we were doing or where we were going, as was completely normal in those days. Sometimes we went out into the fields amongst the horses, where we would meet gangs of boys and girls from other estates. There were phony wars with insults flying and sticks to threaten each other. Mostly we were madly curious about each other and we would hang out in trees talking until it was time to go home to eat.

I don't know how we knew to go home for dinner in the middle of the day. At some point, we would scatter and get fed meat, veg and loads of new spuds with butter. In no time we would be sent on our way and turfed out on the road to play again.

Often we were out late into the summer evenings. Our dad would appear at the latest possible moment and start bellowing for us to come in immediately. We would be loath to go home, but there was always tomorrow.

We used to pester the delivery men. It was common for

lads to be hanging out of the milk float helping the Milkman on his rounds. The Vegetable Man, as we knew him, often took us in his van if there was space. We would go spinning all over Dublin. Again our parents had no idea that we were bouncing around amongst sacks of carrots and peering into other people's gardens around the city.

We once got home late from some jaunt to be met by Dad with a very unhappy face. I can only imagine now how scary that would have been for him, but to us he was a bit of a nuisance trying to cramp our style.

My family and Sean's got up to plenty of mischief during the time we lived near each other. One day 'borrowing' materials from the builders on site to make our own dens, to another day traipsing to the corner shop to buy far too many sweets when we had a few pounds from the visiting aunties. Those free-spirited wild kids were amongst the most wonderful I ever played with, but of course soon we would be leaving them behind too.

DREAMING

After moving into our new house, I found a children's green leather prayer book wrapped up in brown paper in the kitchen. It was a gift from Nanan, Addie's mother. I sat on the bed in my new bedroom, flicking through those parchment leafy pages with the golden edges. I adored this prayer book and I became engrossed in it.

During that summer I developed a very painful bout of

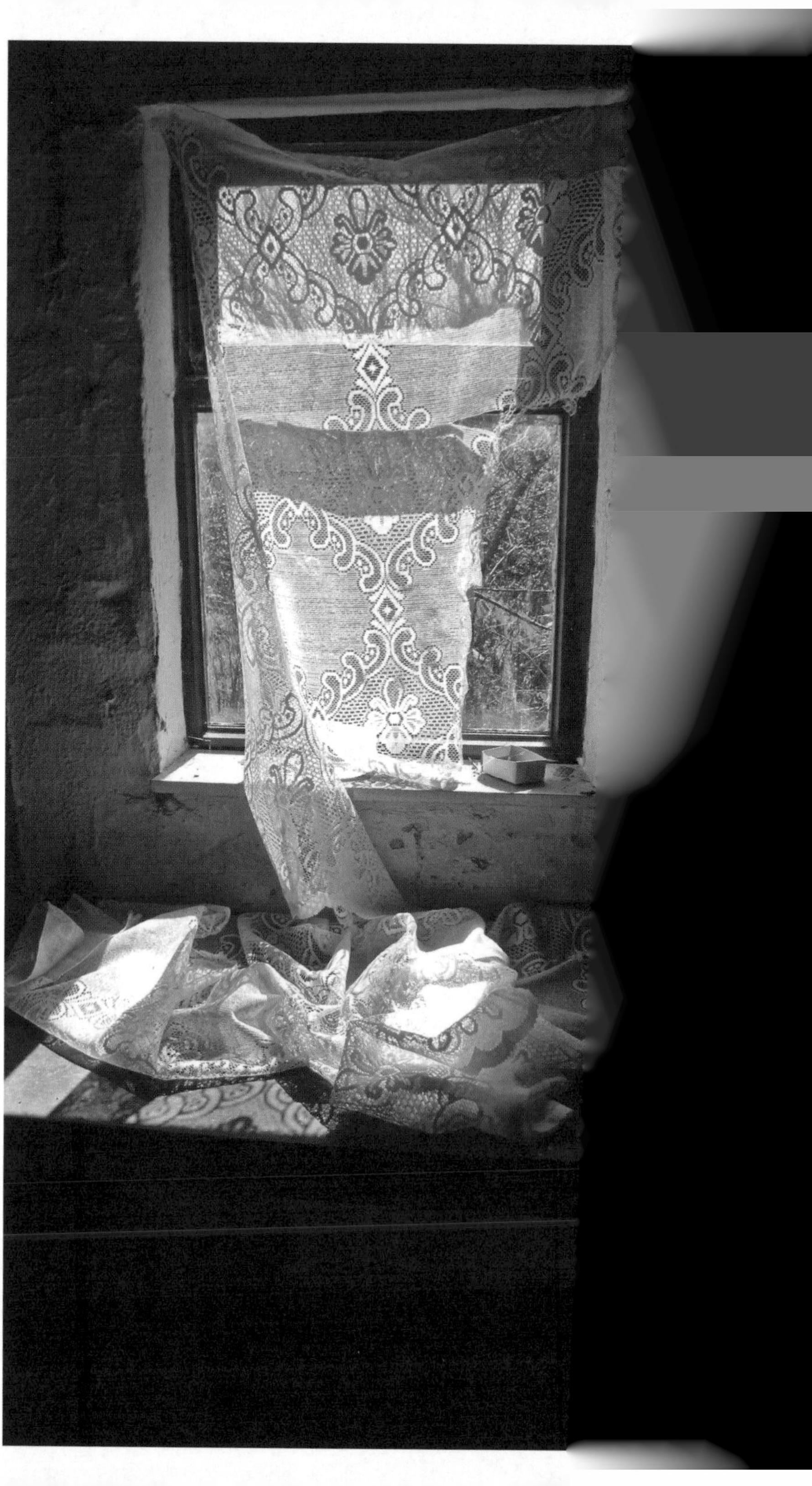

tonsillitis and was confined to bed, delirious at times. I didn't know if I was dreaming, awake or asleep. In my hallucinations women were keening and saying the rosary in the corner of the room. I got up and walked towards them, but when I got there they disappeared.

At some point during my delirium I went to use the bathroom, but when I opened the bathroom door my dad was standing there, holding Addie over a blood-stained basin. I stood there in frozen, feverish shock to see red blood in such quantities. Three times he shouted my name, telling me to go back to bed, but I was stuck to the spot in shock. That was when I realised that something really bad was going on. I couldn't put any words on this feeling of dread, so instead I took out my special prayer book and started to pray.

Years later, my Nanan took me up to the room where I was born and had almost died after days of Addie's hard labour. It was a sunny July day, with warm light pouring in through the large window from the street. 'The midwife had to resuscitate you there when you were finally born,' said Nanan, pointing to a table in the corner of the room. Nanan said that it was here she had prayed, said the rosary over me and then held me after I took my first breath.

I knew this was what had happened even as she was telling me as I had lived it at the time. A memory of this room and my birth had lingered somewhere in the core of my being. The body remembers — that scarcity of breath, the light through the window and the keening women praying over me was an image that would often come to me in dreams.

REMEMBERING TO FORGET

I never talked to anyone about death or the fear of losing Addie at that time. From then on I couldn't find the words for most of what was going on in our house. Home was now a place of anxiety. The kids' tribe distracted me as much as possible and life on the streets of Dublin in the summer of 1963 was enthralling.

Once I ran into the house for a ball, racing upstairs, in and out of every room looking for it. In a lapse from my total denial about what was going on, I ran into the room where Addie lay dying. She was tiny and alone in a huge double bed. In front of her was the wardrobe with a full-length mirror and later my aunt said to me that Addie had literally watched herself fade away through her own reflection.

Addie turned her head very, very slowly as I came to a sudden stop. I was rooted to the spot, terrified by what I

saw, a gaunt shadow and someone I just couldn't see as that girl I knew. She was almost a corpse. We held each other's frightened gaze for a moment or two. I don't know why, but neither of us spoke, and I ran out of the room again, down the stairs and back into the streets, hardly able to breathe.

So thorough was the denial that I went back out to the game as if nothing had happened. Having no way to understand what was going on, I decided that Addie was just very sick, although underneath there was deep gnawing terror. All I could do was pray that she wouldn't die, which I did constantly.

Relatives came and went. There were discussions about Addie's care, arguments, confusion, mostly there was grief and denial. There could be no reassurances given to anyone, how could there be? All anyone knew was that there would be worse to come.

GRACE'S PREMONITION

It was my little sister Grace who had the premonition about Addie's final disappearance. She had dreamt that Addie was eaten by cannibals, or that she had cracked and fallen apart like the pictures of old frescoes in the family bible. She told me all this as we sat on the stairs munching banana sandwiches.

I looked after, played with and slept with Grace in a big double bed. She was sometimes very frightened by her recurring nightmares. She would wake in the night, or when she told the dream she would start to cry. Something or someone was eating Addie up. I knew she was right. Before Addie

even knew herself what exactly was ravaging her body, we felt it. It was as if a dark cloud hung over our world.

We played games to distract ourselves. I would draw pictures on the wooden bedhead of the double bed we shared. I used the sharp end of a hair clip to carve religious figures into the varnish. Jesus dying on the cross in the middle, on either side the two bad men, any number of fairies, flying through the sky or sitting on toadstools just above the pillows.

'And what's that?' G would ask. 'That's Queen of the Faeries with a big stiff skirt and see-through wings.' My biggest fan would be mesmerised.

In my own dreams and nightmares I would see us as refugees wandering out the gate with small suitcases of all we possessed. I probably didn't know much about refugees, except for pictures of war-torn countries in Europe after the Second World War. We were all transfixed by warnings of too many imminent disasters, including a nuclear holocaust that the world was in training for.

Being a refugee was to experience a cruel and painful separation and this anxiety felt exactly like that to me. As refugees we were about to be thrust into the wide world, relying only on the kindness of strangers. I prayed and prayed with great gusto that Addie wouldn't die.

Heaven

Being alert and aware of life inevitably leads to questions about death. When summer ends there is a tinge of sadness, but there is a wonderful golden beauty in it too. As the summer of 1963 faded, so too did darling Addie.

In those days nothing could possibly prepare a child for the death of a mother, so the adults didn't even try. Death was familiar territory to the older generation who had lived through two world wars, the Spanish flu epidemic and the deaths of other children and parents brought about by TB. They were stoical, Victorian even, in their acceptance of death. But they carried grief like a heavy stone on their shoulders.

Children like us knew nothing of death but the fear of it. People went to heaven when they died. I tried to imagine heaven; it was a place with sweet shops and diving boards into blue heated swimming pools; a blue sky every day and the ability to fly.

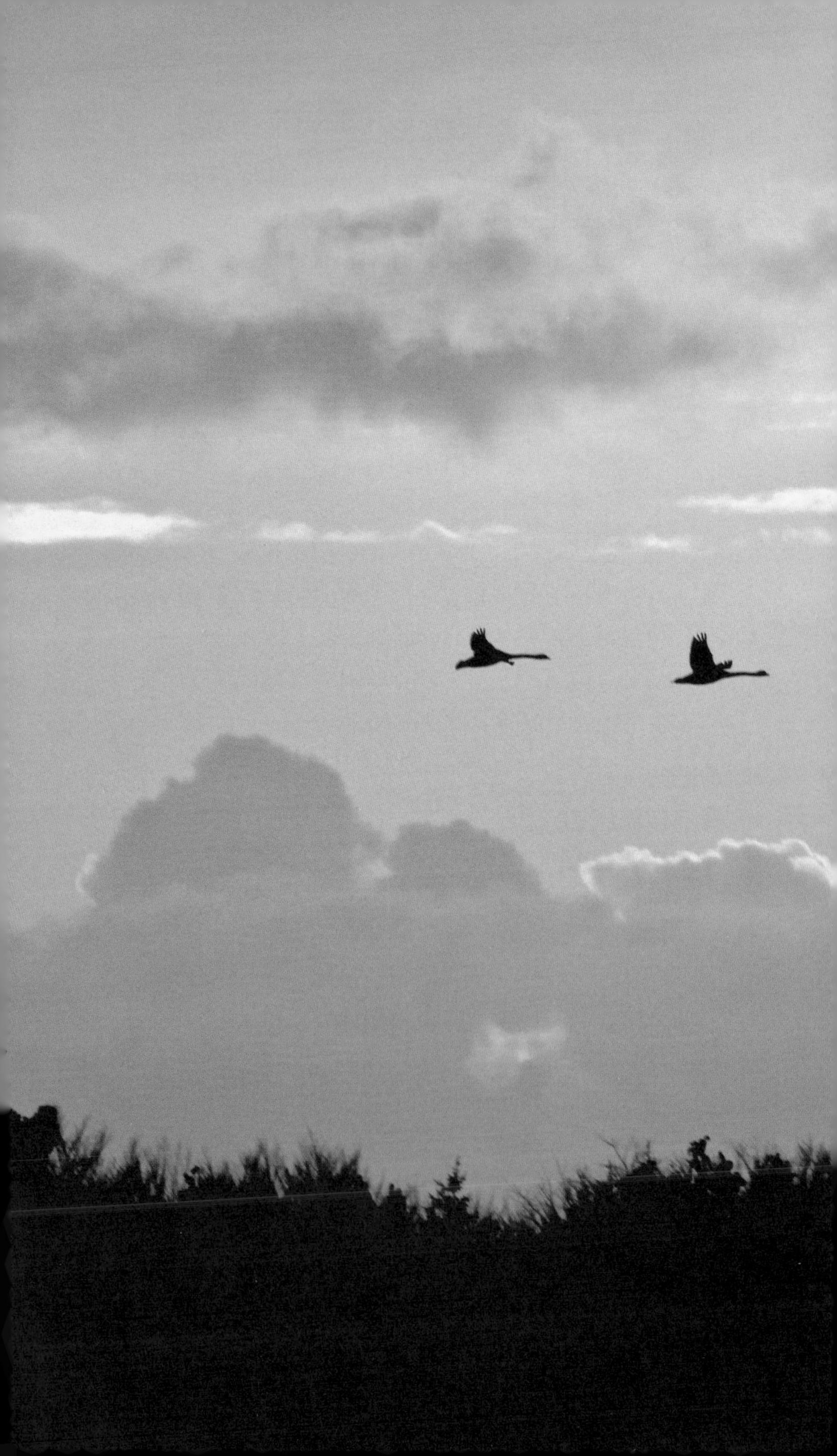

AUTUMN

— Twists and turns along the path —

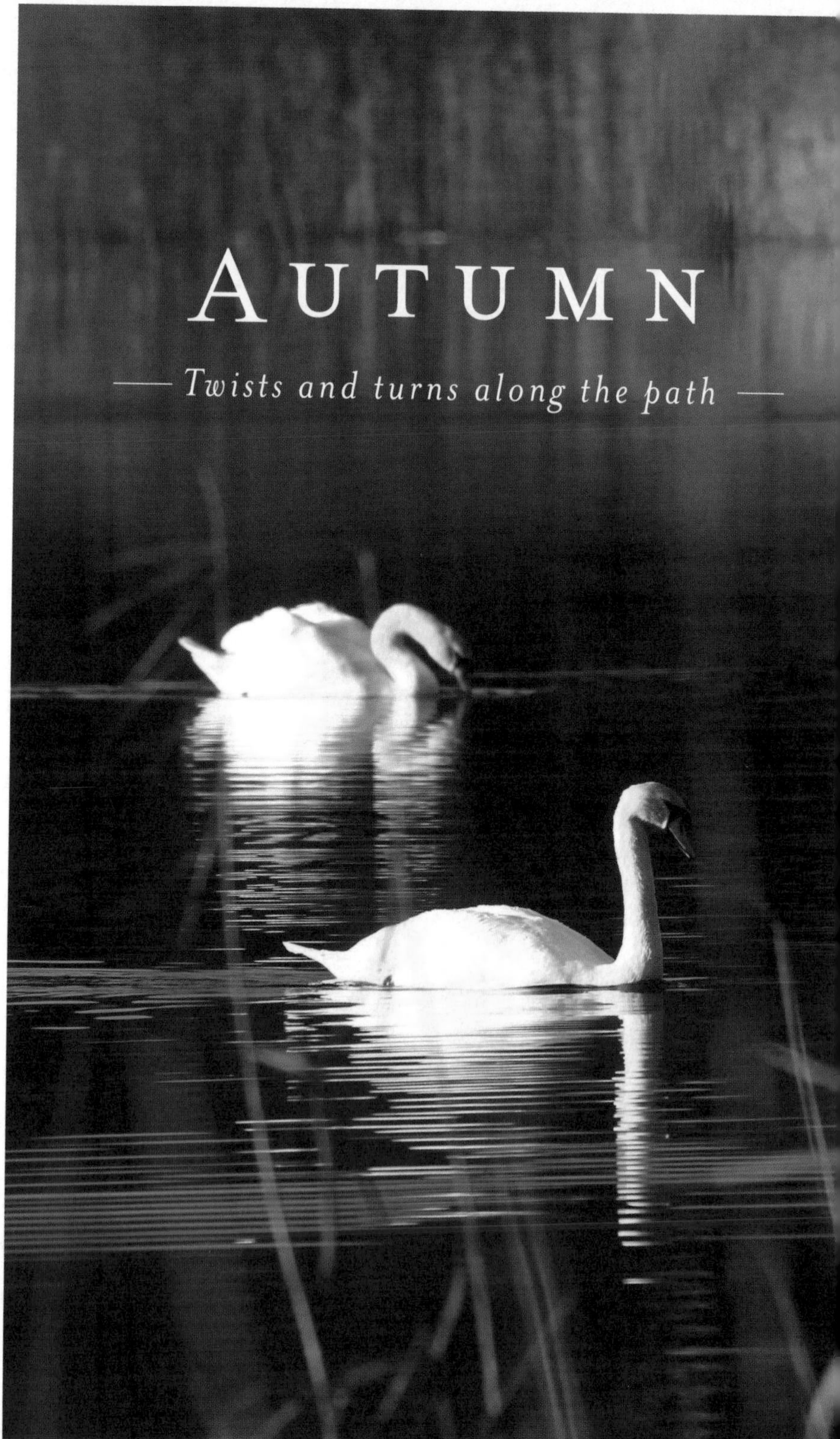

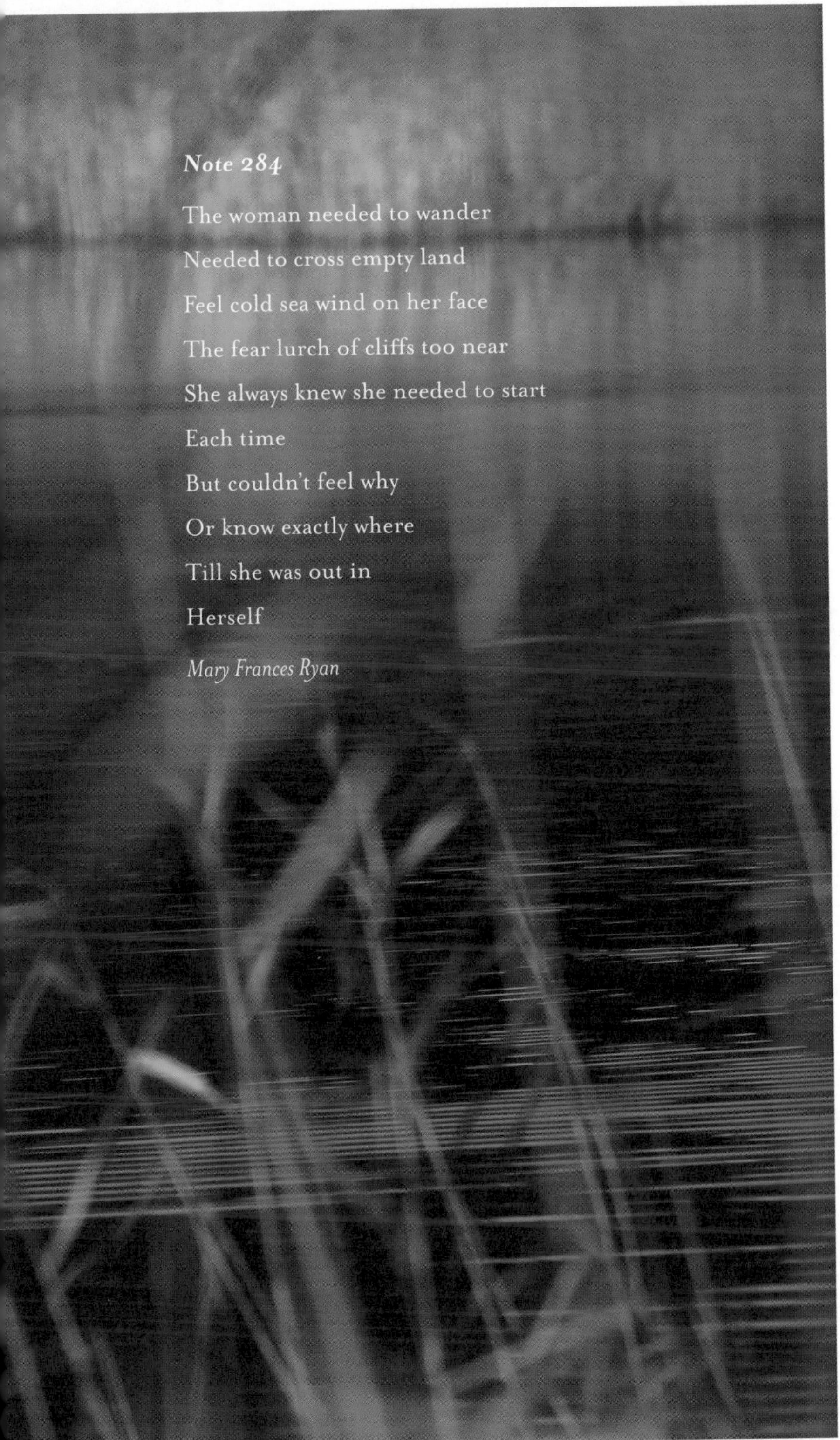

Note 284

The woman needed to wander
Needed to cross empty land
Feel cold sea wind on her face
The fear lurch of cliffs too near
She always knew she needed to start
Each time
But couldn't feel why
Or know exactly where
Till she was out in
Herself

Mary Frances Ryan

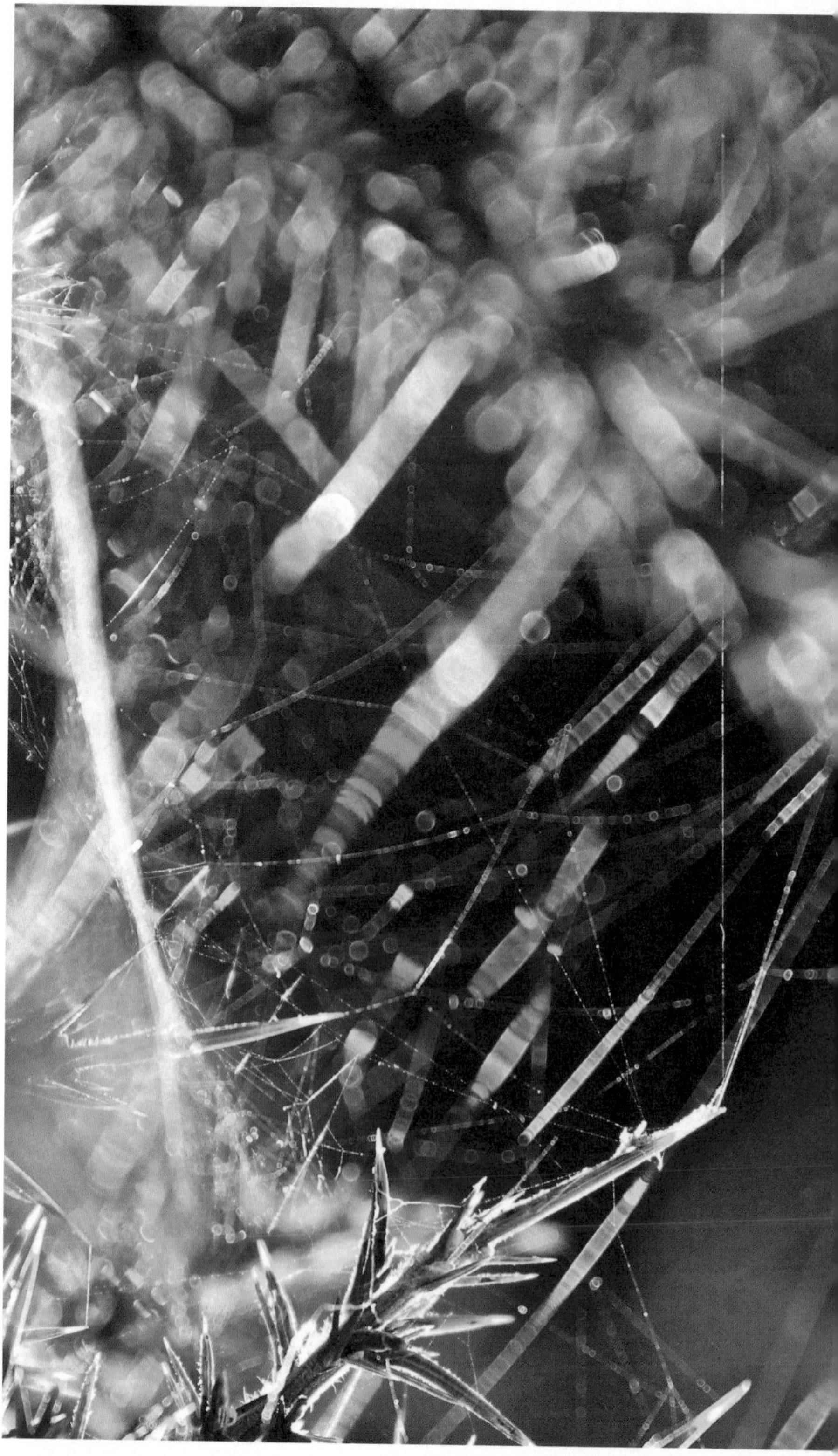

Chapter 9

Seeking light

LIGHT

Autumn is a time of the year when my rambles turn golden. The turning sometimes feels like another lesson in letting go. All around us nature leads the way as leaves separate from their mother ship and float into oblivion.

More than anything, it's this dappled autumn light and how it falls at different times of the day that keeps me pondering the movements of the planet. It took time to grasp reading light in terms of the Earth moving as opposed to the sun moving. The sun is motionless in the sky; it is we who are orbiting the sun, hurtling through the universe at about 1,000 miles (1,600 kilometres) per hour!

In the mornings we are angled towards eastern light and in the evenings turn away towards the dark side. In autumn the light takes on this golden tinge as the atmosphere thickens when we turn a little more on our axis. In winter when the days are shorter, even low grey light creates a neutral template for seeing the true colours of our Irish landscapes. Light is everything. Instead of just looking at objects, on these solitary walks, I gradually learned to look at how the light falls on or around them.

By using a camera, a phone or even a small magnifying glass, ordinary things come to life as you watch light play with them. Walking the tracks and trails, I often find myself standing still for an age waiting for some light to bounce or hoping that the earth will turn and move out from underneath a shadow. Repetition and practice is how we learn and deepen our ability to really see and feel light.

Consistently observing how light interacts with the world is to experience being more present and part of it all. Give light a hundred per cent commitment from eye, hand and heart, and between you, the subject and the light some alchemy happens. Photographers share many of these precious moments of awareness by just being there waiting, bathed in the beauty of it. Photography practice is fundamentally a fascination with light and shade.

A TURNING POINT

One day I overheard one of the aunties on the phone in the hall. She was telling my father to come home immediately that Addie was dying. This was early September and so our first days in the new school would be delayed for weeks.

Instead, we were packed off to Sandycove to stay with the two Dublin aunts and not a mention was made of a death or a funeral. With my child's antennae on full alert I wondered anxiously if it was all over. It would be days before we were told that 'Addie had gone to heaven'. I knew the minute I saw Dad walking up the narrow path of the aunts' house with a handful of ice-cream cones.

Without doubt, Addie's death was a crucial turning point in our lives and it's hard to know how we kids survived after that. While I may have been a slightly introverted and bookish child, after Addie went, I added the trait of being guarded. I became known as Mouse by the aunties and spent a lot of time curled up behind the sofa reading, drawing or just listening to the grown-ups chat.

In those days I don't think children were given credit for having much intelligence. I used to wonder, in all serious-ness, why adults were so blind to our ability to understand life. In fairness, the adults around me were grieving and bereft, so I don't blame any of them; they were doing their best to cope. Everyone missed Addie terribly.

My father, in particular, was at rock bottom. He smoked a lot of cigarettes and stared into the distance mournfully. He never recovered the ability to talk about Addie very much and now that most of his generation are gone, I will never fully know how any of them felt or how they found solace in their grief.

For us four girls under the age of nine, life went on. On the first day in the new Dublin school I was asked many times if I was the girl whose mother had died. Every time I said, 'No!' In my deep confusion I felt that Addie's death was blanketed in what I can only describe as shame. Also being someone who hates being the centre of attention, I dearly wanted to be like all the other kids and fade into the background. It's never easy to be the exotic 'new girl' or the centre of some tragic story.

There were no words to express our family's grief or how unsettling it was to be living in a one-parent household. My way of dealing with the indescribable feelings was to cover them up in an outer shell of normality. Our wounded dad tried his best to get on with life. In later years I was able to admit that my first thought on hearing about Addie's death was 'Oh no, we are going to be left with Dad!' I knew only too well his incompetence in the domestic sphere and his lack of knowledge about the preferences of girls.

Home became a fairly haphazard place. Some of the

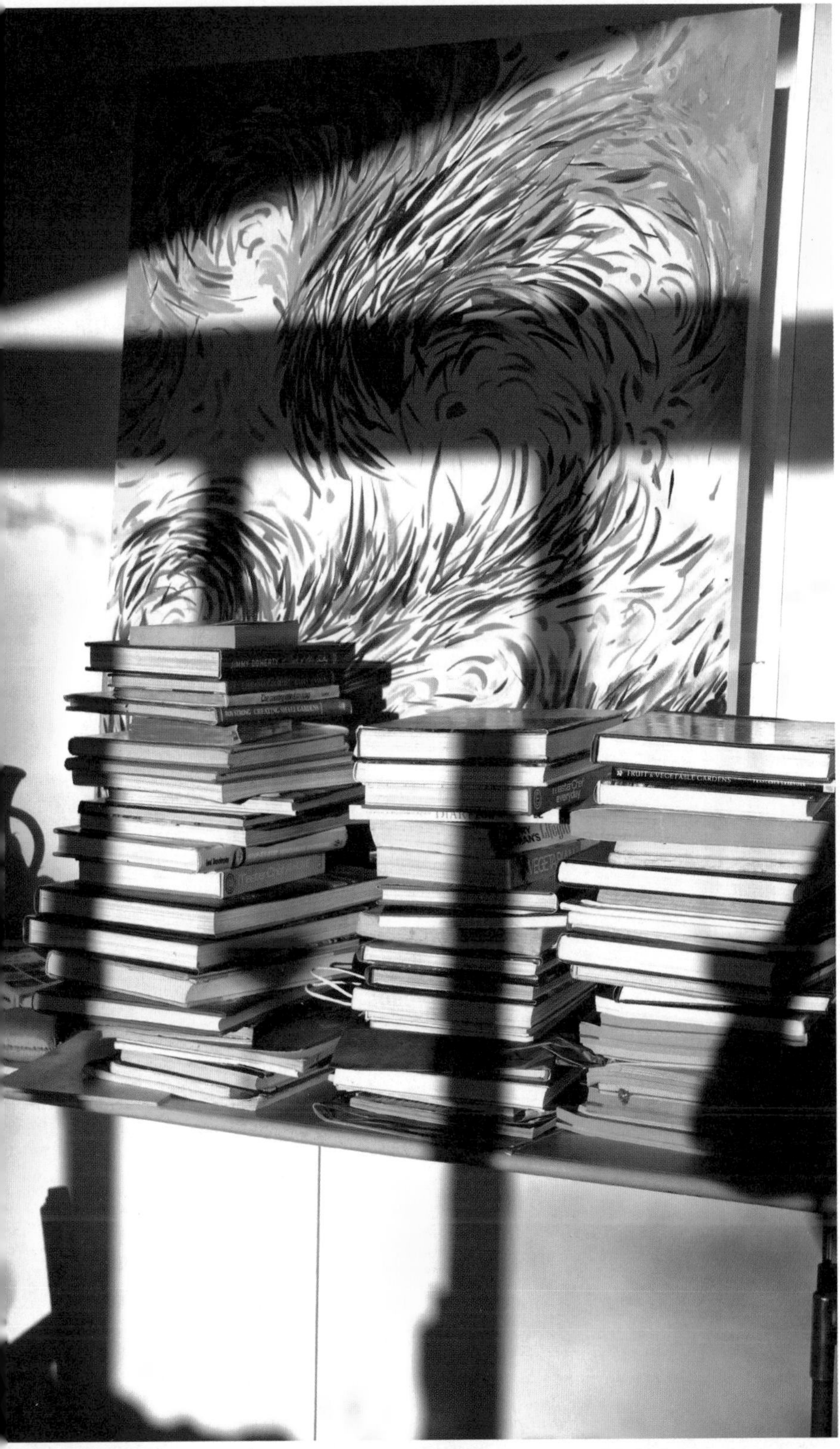
FRUIT & VEGETABLE GARDENS

aunties wanted us to be sent to a boarding school, but Dad wouldn't hear of it as his own boarding school experience was one of the unhappiest in his life. Keeping us all together and safe was heroic for a man to do in those days. As a result, our gang of four sisters has always been a very tight group and we loved our dad dearly in spite of our intimate knowledge of his obvious flaws.

Childminders came and went. School was a fantastic distraction, and new friends and their parents helped to create some kind of community around us. My new best friend and her family became a kind of sanctuary in my small world. We shared a love of Enid Blyton and the Just William books and on a Saturday would go wandering through the park to exchange our large hardback library books, perhaps taking in a quick confession at the church on the route home. It would be many years later that the grief of those years would finally surface and we would all find healing.

THE GIFT

On my tenth birthday, Dad gave me a tiny Instamatic camera. It contained a black-and-white film cassette with twelve shots on it. I patiently eked out each click of the shutter and found a little piece of heaven in the magic of capturing those moments.

This gift of capturing the world through my own lens has given me a lifetime of pleasure. Something special started to happen through the repetitive practice of making

pictures. Time would stand still when I was out and about with the camera, although most of the time I was just looking through the viewfinder and photographing nothing! In particular, over recent years the camera and I have become almost inseparable.

Those first twelve exposures on my tiny camera feature a tired-looking Dad, three little sisters as the perfect models and the kids next door with their dogs and kittens. The limits of that simple camera were frustrating as I had visions of taking hundreds of images and especially taking photos of faraway scenes. The palaver of bringing the film to the pharmacist, waiting for weeks for the return of prints and the ridiculous expense meant that I never had enough film. I had to wait many years until digital photography opened up the possibilities of snapping whatever and whenever.

The beauty of modern technology is the widespread ability to carry a camera with you anywhere. While there is a lot of negativity about social media and phone obsession, the availability of such a portable camera, notebook, research tool, is beyond my generation's wildest dreams.

I remember, as a child, playing futuristic games where we imagined just touching a button and a cinema screen would appear at the end of your bed. Or maybe flicking a switch and turning on any music you could conjure up. Or having a robot who you could order around to do your bidding. Maybe my generation, more than any, finds joy and possibility in owning one of these magical little devices.

So when the endless possibilities of digital photography opened up and on a boring wet Sunday I posted a photo of a wild foxglove online, in this one move I had become a photoblogger.

Moving on

Over time, it was almost like Addie had never existed. We moved house again, leaving the green fields and deep friendships we had made. Except for some furniture made by her father and the rose tea set, everything that had belonged to Addie was lost in that move. Everything except for the long, shot-silk evening dress and silver sandals that we used to dress up in until it too disappeared.

Many years later, I was in a lift in a hotel in Taiwan when

an Irish man walked into the lift on the 11th floor. As the lift descended we performed the Irish ritual of trying to find out what would eventually connect us. When he heard my name, he stopped and said, 'I think I bought a house from your father.' He had indeed bought that house where Addie had died. Then when I heard his name, I knew immediately that he had also taught my Right-Hand Man at school. We were connected all right. As we left the building, each going our separate ways, he shook my hand and looked into my eyes. 'Very sad, it was, very sad.'

Number 73 would be our last move until we each left home and made our own way. The house was a stone's throw from the new school with the green uniforms that I had longed to go to the day I saw a crowd of girls queuing up at a bus stop. We could hop over the back wall, cross a ploughed field, go down a driveway and we would be there. There was a resident farmer on the school grounds, a horse called Dolly and a

walled garden of apple trees. On the front lawn was a droop-
ing ash and I made pencil drawings of its autumn leaves and
huge branches. One of my first creative projects there was
a puppet show of *Alice in Wonderland*, where we made all the
puppets and sets ourselves. I had a very small part as Bill the
Lizard and I spent days forming him from papier mâché and
lashings of green paint.

I loved that school, and for a lost child the sense of belonging to a community was immediate solace. Our classroom
was in a tall converted residence at the front gate of the main
school. There, I saw for the first time a nature table and was
fascinated by the plants and their names. There was also a
large front garden where we undertook weeding duties and
planted seedlings. Mostly I disappeared with Alice down the
rabbit hole and did my best to be normal.

Sisters

Four girls under one roof was both a blessing and a curse
to a nine-year-old eldest child. I can list all the mishaps
that happened to my toys and clothes, and the many outings
where I had to 'bring your little sister' or else.

My precious American doll, although given a radical crew
haircut by myself, was certainly not improved by a blue biro
scribble all over her very American face. The best friend who
lent me her grandmother's fragile storybook was horrified to
find it was eventually dug up from the bottom of the garden,
having been left out in all weathers by a couple of toddlers.

The new top that I bought for some special occasion had already been worn and stained.

Grace was now making all her own friends too. She adored babies and small children, so would pick up and cuddle any child. Today, a grandmother herself she is still at the heart and soul of our family, although she lives in Sweden. Mary, two years younger, was always busy. She made little shops out of paper and dolls house furniture. She created a post office in the back bedroom that was the envy of all and is still a crafter and maker with magic hands. Quiet and with the biggest brown eyes, we all thought she was as pretty as her favourite doll that we decided was an Italian girl.

Melanie, two years younger again, was destined to always be the baby of the family, whether she liked it or not. Dark-haired, like Addie, she was sweet and loving as a child. She adored animals, having an especially close rapport with dogs and still lives with at least two at any one time. I think Dad was especially connected to her and she seemed to bring out the best of his parenting abilities.

We were always close, but each of us sought out our own individual path of solace. Part of that has been our enduring sisterhood, the sharing of our particular family experience and growing up together through all the confusion and loss. Although I left home first, there were many times when we laughed at ourselves or commiserated over some disaster or other. We still talk most days and I don't think anything could ever come between us or our commitment to each other and all of our children. It wasn't easy to grow up in our house as grief hung over us at times, but each of us found our own way of muddling through as we grew up.

After Addie's death when adults gathered us in, it was usually in their own sorrow. I couldn't understand at the time why they would start to cry or turn away in sadness when they saw us. Sometimes one of them would hug and cling on like there was no letting go. I don't think we displayed 'proper grief' so everyone probably assumed we were all grand. Of course the inner grief of a child takes many forms and adults don't always read the signals.

By the time the American president John F Kennedy was assassinated in November of 1963, it had been one bereavement after another in our family: Addie, her brother-in-law, her nephew, and also her beloved aunt who she was named after. The outpouring of grief about a dead American president provided an outlet for our family. I cut out photos from the newspapers of JFK's children at the funeral and created a grim scrapbook of assassination facts. The nation became obsessed with the wall-to-wall coverage, and JFK's death became a catharsis of sorts as sherry was poured and tears were shed.

The trauma we were all handling was acute. Our dad was totally devastated and did his best to pretend otherwise. No one knew anything about counselling or the five stages of grief then, far from it, it was just a case of getting on with things.

After that, our family would always be stuck in Stage 1, Denial. We all had become experts at it.

THE MYSTERY OF DAD

Dad and I formed a bit of a team after Addie died. Although in fairness my assessment of Dad was that he was very much the junior partner in this arrangement. I had no idea how any of us were ever going to thrive in his care.

Dad was going to be playing Father and Mother to four girls under nine and in my opinion was clueless about girls.

Kids know stuff, but we didn't understand grief in all its forms. Dad just seemed to be in bad humour a lot of the time. It took years for me fully to understand the trauma he was going through in those days.

Dad then was as much a mystery to me as I was to him. Back in the Rose-Petal Garden days, when me and Dad would be flying through the countryside on his big black bike, he would suddenly become a rule breaker. Then he was like another kid, going faster and faster into the wind, screaming out loud and giggling at the risk. Dad after Addie's death was preoccupied, distant, morose.

Many years later when he was going through his last autumn with us he used to clutch my hand and say, 'I was a terrible father.' *Yes you were*, I sometimes wanted to say, but instead I would say, 'No you weren't, you were brilliant,' and I knew by then that it was true.

Becoming a swimmer

I began to pester Dad about Butlin's Holiday Camp when I first saw the ads on TV. It was really the glorious swimming pool that caught my eye: turquoise blue with coloured streamers and toys hanging from the roof.

The only indoor swimming pool I had ever encountered up until then was the old Iveagh Baths in Dublin. Here, you could dip in and out of a freezing cold hole in the grey, hard

concrete. It was one of two cold pools in the inner city, and often local children would come in with bars of soap as it was probably their only means of having a wash.

At ten years old, my dream was to learn to swim properly.

Eventually, due to mounting pressure, Dad sent away for a Butlin's brochure and myself and the other kids drooled over it. Butlin's Mosney was virtually on the beach. You could spend all day going from one fun activity to another. You could get free rides on any number of hurdy gurdies and best of all you would stay in your own little house and have every meal catered for in a giant cafeteria.

The brochure just increased the pressure on poor Dad. He would look at me, saying nothing while I pleaded my case. Then he would stare kind of longingly into space. I can only imagine now that the poor man was trying to weigh up the two sides of this decision. The kids would have a ball, yes, but he must have been thinking about the long days and nights on his own with four girls under ten, including a baby still in nappies.

Pleeeeeeease we begged. On and on I ranted about learning to swim and how I would mind my sisters and maybe he could play golf? All the things I thought might offer up an attractive proposition.

In the end, he gave in, and soon the promise of going on holidays to Butlin's was the most exciting item on the agenda in our house. We counted the days until we would set off, practising swimming by lying down in the grass, holding our breath and doing the breaststroke around the garden.

Aunties stepped up to the plate and provided dresses. Mine was described by my fashionable aunt as a 'tent dress'. She had made it herself out of bright orange fabric with enormous flowers on it. She showed me something very similar designed by Mary Quant in a magazine. Yep! I got the jist.

While most of that precious holiday is a blur, I did actually learn to swim. Dad, fairly typically, messed up the final triumphant moment when I was to receive my certificate. We were late and I had to do the lengths of the pool on my own to get the approval of the coach. No matter what, I just had to have that certificate! In fact, due to more of Dad's incompetence, I never got my cert, and obviously never forgot it either.

Our days were spent going from the pool to the toy-car roundabout. This turned out to be our favourite ride. You could sit in tiny cars and pretend you were driving while they went around in circles. Grace and myself were totally charmed by it.

Listening to Dad years later moaning to anyone who would listen, about his week of hell in Butlin's Holiday Camp with four little girls, I could never fully believe that we had been to the same idyllic place. Bleating on about how he was the only man nappy-washing in the washeteria, having to eat what he called 'square' meals, and all the late nights with a wakeful baby and sunburnt kids.

There were no lone parents in those days, or none that we knew of anyway. My dad was a single man marooned in holiday heaven amongst a horde of happy families. At night he would sneak out to the bar while I rubbed calamine lotion on the sisters' sunburnt little bodies. Those mornings after the night before, when the sun poured in, would prove to be the bane of his existence.

'Dad! Dad! Wake up! I can hear the loudspeaker. Breakfast is ready!'

Out cold to the world, our champion, legend of a dad would groan, clutch his forehead and mutter, 'Right, get your shoes on, off we go … again.'

DROWNING IN LOSS

As the years moved on, Addie became a feeling rather than a proper memory. How the warmth of the sun stretched up our hallway and reached my toes as I sat on the bottom step of that stairs. How I would wiggle my feet in and out of this shaft of summer sun or try to catch a butterfly flapping against the glass of the hall door. Squinting at the light

filling the stairwell until I put down my copybook and lay there in the glow, listening to Addie's playing.

I feel now that this memory of Addie was with me the day I almost drowned in Dublin Bay. When in my panic I began to fill my lungs with seawater as I struggled to breathe or cry out. How I slipped beneath the surface, no longer able to doggie paddle, losing the light and the sounds of children splashing and swimming above me. How my feet couldn't find any solid ground as I had slipped off the pier and was out of my depth. There was nothing to hold on to; I was to be lost at sea in the warm light that flashed in the swell around me.

Suddenly I was grabbed by a large man. Maybe he was a father swimming with his children or an experienced swimmer who kept an eye out for children like me, failing to understand the limits of the shallow waters. Could he have been a lifeguard? Having shaken me upside down and stood me up, asking if I was OK, the man brought me to where my grieving dad was sitting on a rug, smoking and staring into the distance as he habitually did.

Few words were said. Dad didn't admit that he might have messed up by forgetting about me in the water. We sat on the rug in silence, each in our own bewilderment. Me, thinking I am truly alone here and for that reason I will have to become a much better swimmer. And Dad feeling the weight of responsibility and dread at his overwhelming role in life — a widower with four young daughters in a world full of danger.

MAY

Three years after Addie died, Dad brought May home to meet us. May was beautiful with a big smile and she sat anxiously on the edge of her seat while Dad went to make tea. As soon as he was out of the room, the sisters jumped on top of her with one question, 'Can we see your false teeth?'

May's smile was all her own and one night Dad sat on the edge of my bed and showed me the gold wedding ring that he had just bought for her. Although I was a bit unsure of what all this meant, Dad enthusiastically sold the whole endeavour when he told me that May had her own red mini car and that she would bring us to the beach whenever we wanted.

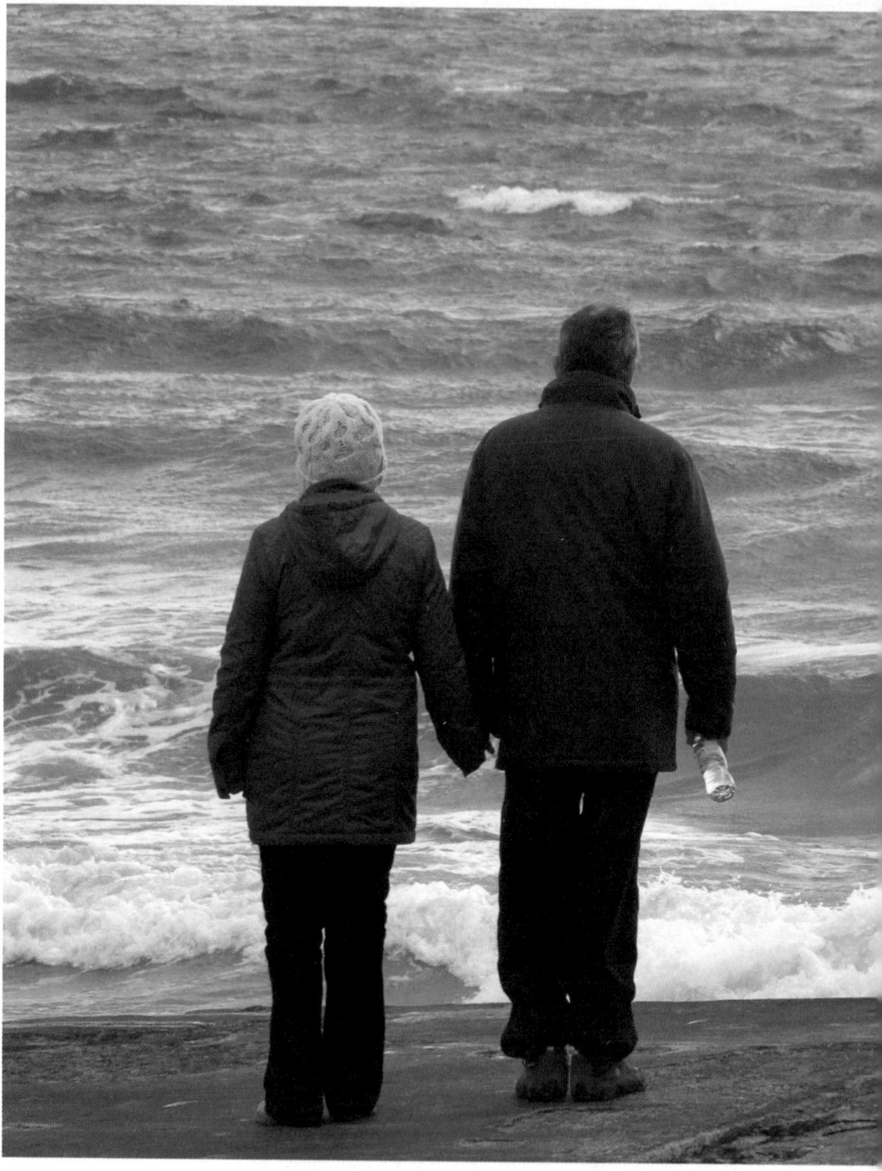

As it turned out, May didn't like the beach at all and was far more at home wandering on a green country lane.

The main outcome for the girl-with-no-mother was that I soon became notorious as the girl-who-went-to-her-own-father's-wedding. There were absolutely no blended families in those days and no language to deal with dead mothers or stepmothers, so it was another case of muddling through.

May loved animals, children and cooking. In my eyes she was a kind of domestic goddess. In a way, she took the burden of responsibility off my shoulders as Dad was deliriously happy and well taken care of for the foreseeable future.

Our much anticipated two new baby sisters were both stillborn and May almost died of a clot after the first birth. Yet again, I turned outwards to the rest of the world to avoid feeling too much of the pain May and Dad went through at that time. I began to send May letters and drawings to cheer her up and found some of them amongst her things when she died.

In her last years she had dementia and our visits with her were full of hysterical laughter and tall tales. She seemed happier at the end than she had been for years. Sadly, at the age of ninety-three, May became one of the first victims of Covid 19. It is still very hard to process it all.

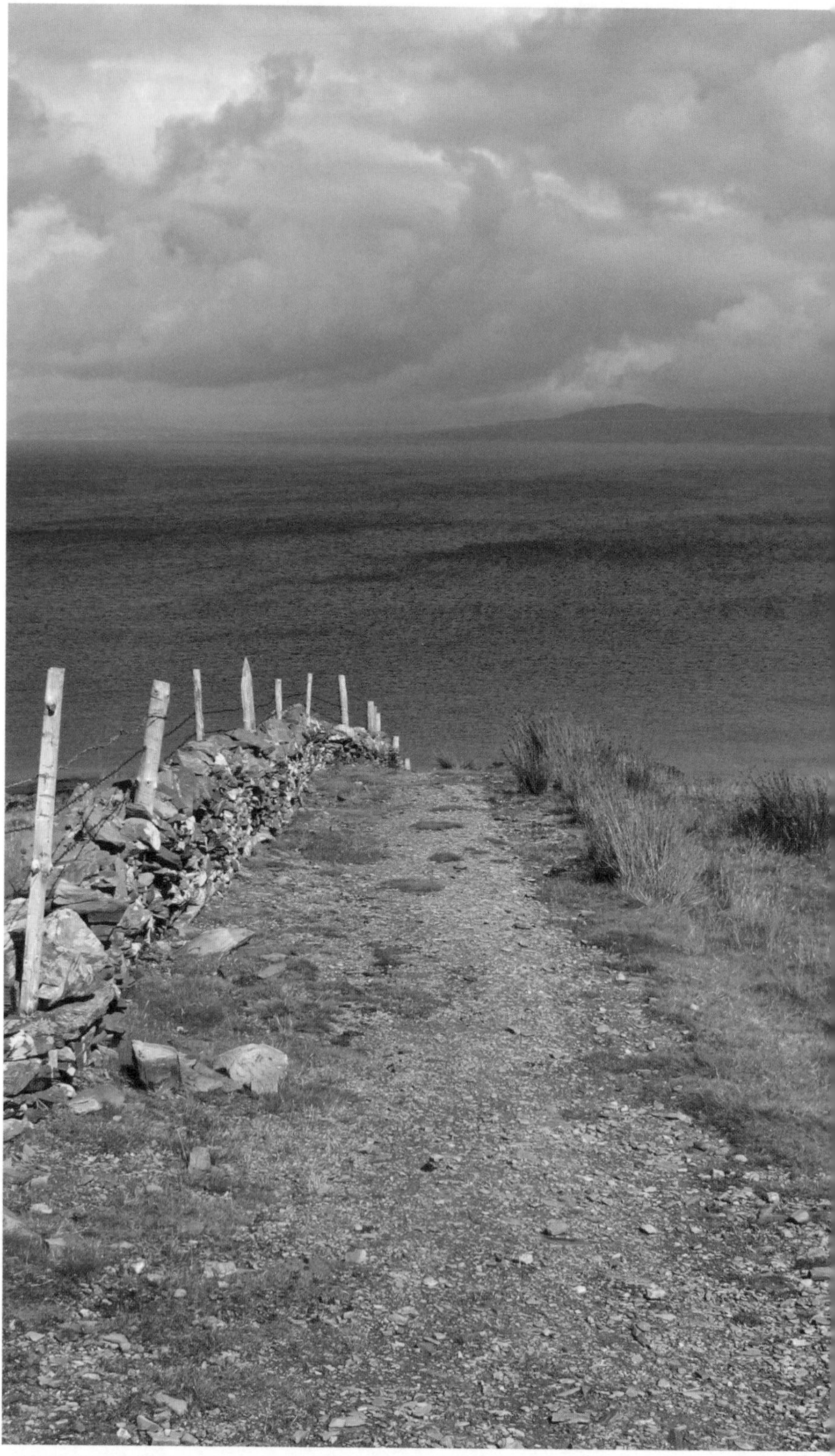

Chapter 10

Wandering further afield

UNCERTAINTY

I t feels these days as if we are living through times that will change forever how we live and define ourselves. As we slowly adjust and with dark news on the horizon there is still a gathering awareness of our global connection as a human species. Have we finally realised that we will not thrive without working as one community?

In the last few years I have felt more 'Earthling' than Irish. The vulnerable and disconnected child in me identifies more with migrants looking for a safe haven than the comfortable tribes who block their desperate passage. Maybe the pandemic experience and days of war will move more of us towards a kinder global oneness.

ESCAPE

As a teenager I walked around Dublin looking for an 'Art College' and was determined not to go to university even though I had a place. There were no courses for 'creative writing' in those days and I couldn't visualise myself composing any more essays on dead poets. I would eventually find my niche and spend ten years in all between a number of colleges over the next years.

In our final year at school we had enjoyed staging *The Playboy of the Western World* by John Millington Synge, who had lived on Inishmaan (*Inis Meáin*) and had been inspired by the Aran Islands. The play was directed by a senior nun who was wickedly mischievous and adored Irish culture. I had been Pegeen Mike in our stage version and two of my friends had played Shawn Keough and the Widow Quin. Just before we would restart our lives in third-level education, the three of us decided to head off to explore the three Aran Islands for a western world adventure and it felt very grown up to be travelling without adults.

We were all heartily seasick on the *Naomh Éanna*, the since-decomissioned island ferry that departed in those days from Galway at an unearthly hour. The lads on board had great amusement describing the salty bacon we would be eating for our breakfast while we held on to each other and lurched. When we got in view of Inisheer (*Inis Óirr*) we were lowered into currachs via an opening beneath the decks and rowed onto the shore.

Our home for the next few days would be a cottage on the beach, with no running water or toilet, and very little to eat, except eggs, mutton and lots of strong 'tae'. The toilet arrangement was in the hen house and part of the ritual involved shooing curious hens away while you attended to business. Our hosts, a young couple, were shy and kept to themselves.

We had our first-ever beer there in the local pub, we met blonde-haired German boys in proper outdoor clothes, the likes of which we had never seen, and we hiked off with them round the island, swimming in our underwear off the rocks.

This was a first taste of travel and freedom and I knew that I wanted more of it. I worked all through college, from waitressing to my coolest job as a live-in caretaker of the Royal Irish Academy in the centre of Dublin. I was determined to be a free spirit and was amongst a lucky generation of young women to challenge some outdated preconceptions about being female.

THE EMIGRATION TRADITION

While I would happily walk my own tracks and trails any day of the week, there is wonder in taking a walk in a new place. The familiar path has a kind of intimacy, but travel allows us the freedom of a fresh view on the world. A change of scene can change everything. After my first trip alone as a young adult I was dying to escape humdrum grey Dublin and run wild and free.

Irish people for generations have travelled the world and I was determined to leave Ireland and join them. Our old black-and-white TV was like a beating drum telling stories about the changes that were coming. I wrote passionate notes in my diary about revolution and women's liberation. Through those years we sat in quaint pubs drinking as many pints of Guinness as we could afford and fantasising about running away to South America. In the end it never happened and a completely different path opened up.

Meanwhile, every opportunity to travel was like a practice run. However the day I left Dublin Airport for New York, I wailed all my way to the departure gate. I had just said goodbye to my Right-Hand Man and when I looked back he was standing there, at the other side of the barrier, weeping. I carried on crying on the plane all the way to New York, but my pals were wise and wonderful and soon I was focused on surviving and getting a job to pay my way in the Big Apple.

To many Irish families familiar with emigration, Munich, Sydney or Chicago are just the next parish. In spite of the sadness of leaving home behind, to be en route to New York in 1979 was bewitching; I was full of anticipation of the iconic architecture, the food, the people. I couldn't wait to explore it all.

NYC

Back in the 1970s, our apartment was to be a sublet on Greenwich Street. The Irish owner was travelling and leaving us her miniscule space with a bedroom, a bathroom and a kitchen-living room. The apartment was infested with cockroaches so our first task was to set up our Roach Motel traps. As the ads on the subway said: 'The roaches check in, but they don't check out!'

Roaches were an entirely new species to us. Soon we got to study them, whether we liked it or not. You would think that they had been eradicated, but at night-time as soon as the lights were switched off more roaches re-emerged and crawled over everything. When the light was turned on again, they scarpered back into the cracks of the ancient building.

On Greenwich Street, in this historic house, we were literally in the shadow of the Twin Towers. Some evenings after dark, we would lie on the roof staring up at the majesty of those buildings and basking in the glow of their night lights. On the ground floor of our building was a cocktail lounge where women danced up and down on the bar. Here we would 'hang' and try fancy cocktails like Tequila Sunrise and Pina Colada.

There were sometimes up to six of us sharing these rooms. We took turns on the bed, usually three on the bed and three on the floor. We never thought twice about this being weird, but were deliriously happy with our cool address.

WORKING THREE JOBS

Every day we wandered around Manhattan looking for work. Even though I knew I shouldn't, I spent all my emergency money going to the movies in an arty twenty-four-hour cinema and visiting the Museum of Modern Art.

My first job was on the ground floor of the Chrysler Building. In the 1930s my grand-uncle worked in the Empire State Building as an elevator operator and I often thought

of him, and my peanut-selling grand-aunt as I dished out yoghurts, desserts and toppings on a long buffet counter. Louis, the guy on beverages, next to me on the line was like everyone else working in NYC — an aspiring actor.

Born and raised in Harlem, Louis tried to educate me on what it was to be young and black in America. There was a popular TV show called *Roots* and this was the closest thing he had to the story of his own heritage. He enlightened me about Kunta Kinte, the main character in the series, and how Africans were stolen from their families and enslaved on Southern plantations.

Monday to Friday I worked during the day in the Yogur-tarian Cafe, at night I went around the corner to waitress in an Italian restaurant serving Fettuccini Alfredo and at week-ends I worked in a Chinese cocktail bar downtown.

After work, the stylish Louis would take us Irish girls, a group of very green art students, on tours of his New York.

Off the beaten track in those days was dangerous and dark. Before New York was 'cleaned up' it was teeming with gangs, had daily murders, and armed cops everywhere. One night I arrived in a subway station where there was an active police chase after an apparent murder. Next day I cut my hair short and started chewing gum, a strategy to look like a tough punk and blend in.

Another evening, while having a drink with friends in a bar on Second Avenue, a truck driver put a bag of cash on the counter, pointed to me and shouted, 'Hey kid, wanna come with me out to California?' The intervention of three other men saw him off. Somehow I took these strange events in my stride, but I kept chewing the gum.

Downtown, we kitted ourselves out with drainpipe cotton trousers and brightly printed Hawaiian shirts. On Friday nights we dressed down and went to CBGBs uptown, to hang out and catch Patti Smith. The place heaved with young punks and the supercool. It felt like the centre of the cultural universe.

THE WINDS OF CHANGE

There's something about coming and going from Ireland that touches the heart. Seeing the shoreline of Ireland disappear into the horizon is one of my favourite experiences. Even still, when taking the ferry away from Rosslare or Cork Harbour, the sense of adventure and belonging to the bigger world feels optimistic and enlightening.

Equally, coming home to Ireland is to be blanketed in familiarity and delight. So many times custom officials have welcomed me home, asked where I was or told me of some fresh local news. But it's the welcoming smile and recognition that warms the heart.

After experiencing the freedom of travel: busking around Germany, hitchhiking to Turkey and singing for my supper in a vegetarian restaurant in Stockholm, it was time to make a number of decisions. For someone anxious for adventure and travel, the world was calling. On the other hand, being newly married and with college to finish, maybe Ireland would be the place to stay for a while more? We were not the only ones weighing up options and facing a bleak outlook; most of our friends had already gone. Staying or leaving, Ireland was breaking my heart.

If we stayed, it was going to be a matter of finding a niche and a way to live with one foot in the mainstream and one foot in a new country of our imagination. We were passionate about change in those days, but when would we ever see it? Myself and my Right-Hand Man had already moved on from any expectations that we would settle into the system and accept the state of the country. I had been glued to the stories about Black Liberation and the Women's Movement. There was no doubt that Ireland would follow, but then it was hard to see exactly how.

Around this time, rural Ireland was becoming a haven for artists moving away from the oppressive straight lines of previous societies. Ireland outside of cities and towns was like another country to us. We muddled on in uncertainty for a while, but in the end the decision to move to rural Ireland made staying easier than we expected. Turned out there was a whole other world waiting.

A FORK IN THE ROAD

In 1979, on the cusp of leaving the country, an unusual opportunity presented itself. A project in rural Kilkenny, made up of community carers, biodynamic farmers and people with special needs, wanted a young architect to come and design homes around these very specific circumstances.

My Right-Hand Man was the architect of choice and the project opened up the chance for us both to live in the country and stay in Ireland for the foreseeable future. While we tried to figure out how to make this work, we visited the project's small biodynamic farm. On our journey back to Dublin

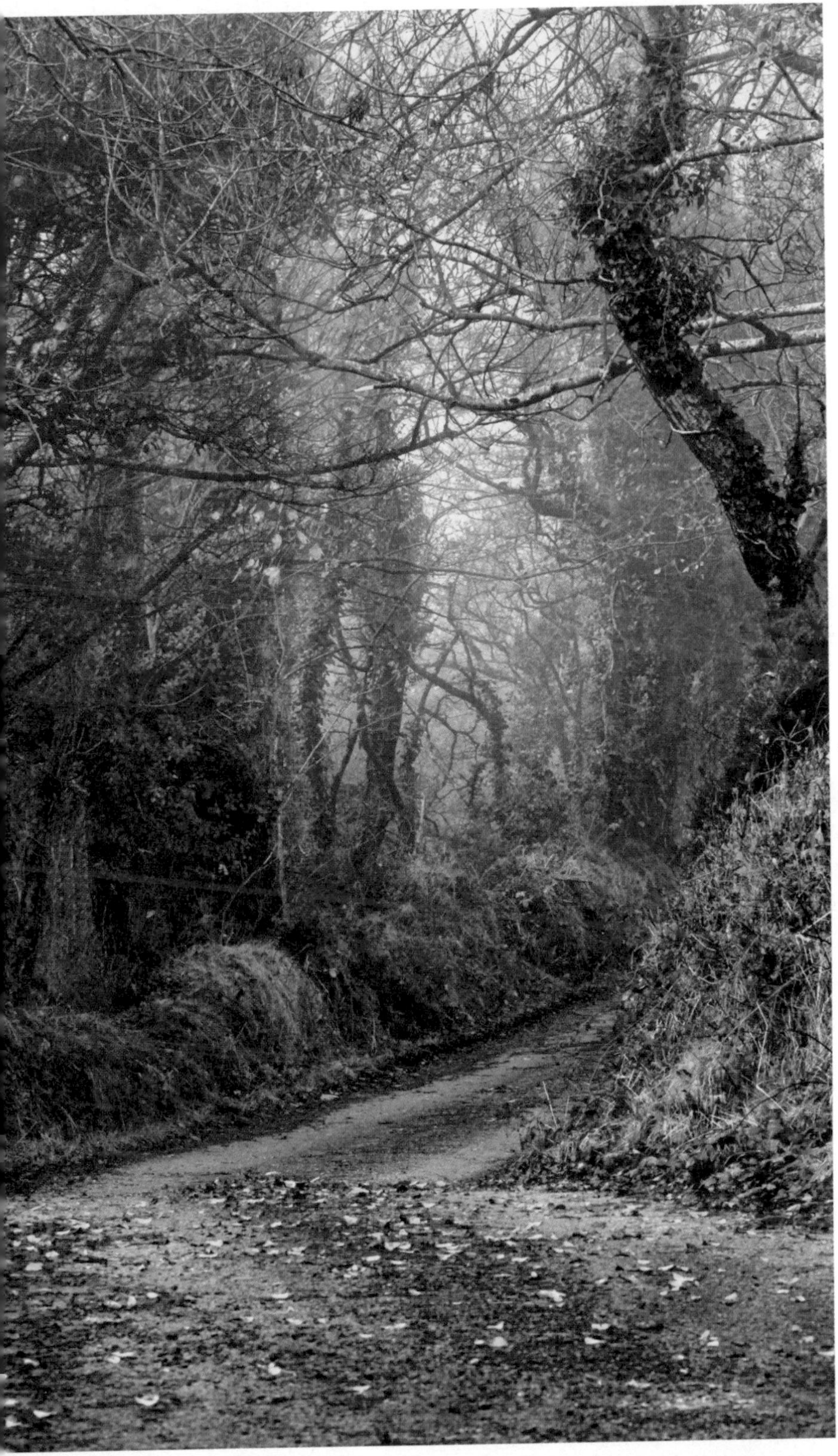

the train got stuck for an hour between stations. In the half light, somewhere between Thomastown and Muine Beag we listed the pros and cons of leaving our lives in Dublin and moving to the country. There were so many things on the pro list that the decision was made for us then and there.

I continued to study at the Art College in Dublin. They permitted me to travel up once a week while I taught art at the local school and worked remotely, which was fairly radical. The Reverend Mother at the local school was also very accommodating and when she once delayed me from catching my train for my weekly trip to Dublin, she simply rang the Station Master in Kilkenny and told him to hold the 11 o'clock for one of her teachers, which he did. As I ran down the platform puffing and panting, the guard raised his eyes to heaven, blew the whistle and we were off. It was very clear who was a person of influence in those days.

Chapter 11

Soulfire

THE WOMEN'S CIRCLES

While the powerful women on all sides of the family were incredible role models, being the girl-without-a-mother still left a vacuum in my life learning. Luckily there have been other strong women in my life who have both loved and challenged me in spite of this blank slate about how to be a proper grown-up woman. Moving to rural Ireland it became a life-saving necessity to have friends and also to be part of the huge changes that were coming down the line. Rural women had tough lives then and low expectations. Over the next fifty years that would change.

Often struggling with figuring out how to get by themselves, other women taught me the importance of rolling up your sleeves and getting stuck in. There was so much to do. It started with workshops, counselling groups, campaigns, marches, seminars, meetings and above all these circles

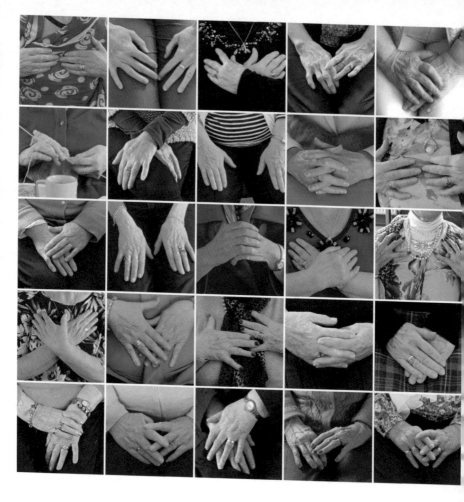

of support where women held each other and allowed the tears to flow. There, we shared stories of births, break-ups, deaths, miscarriages, stillbirths, adoptions and abortions. There was no going back from these truth-telling circles. Deep bonds were created then that have lasted a lifetime.

These women's circles lit a flame in us. Like our activist foremothers, we kept unpicking that old knitted tapestry full of intricacies and knots. We couldn't stop until we had undone them all and began weaving anew.

We were each feeling our own way in an Ireland that would

have preferred us to stay hidden. Each of us, finding ways to be ourselves. We wanted access for all our sisters to what had been denied in the school system, the class system and through generations of exclusion. As the great labour women's song says, we wanted bread and roses too.

COMMUNITY

Women couldn't wait until all the wrongs in Ireland had been sorted out. Even though the odds were against us, we still found ways to succeed in work and family life in spite of the barriers at that time. I had been working for ten years as an art teacher when I began to use art to work with groups in the wider community: young offenders, women's groups, community activists.

Here I had to face up to the devastating conditions that a lot of families were living in during the 1980s. Some of the first women I met were surviving exclusively on social welfare. They had to explain to me the difference between buying a sliced pan or buying a bag of Waterford blaas for breakfast. A bag of blaas (a blaa is a white floury bap) would cost twice as much and would be gone at one meal, whereas a sliced pan would last for the whole day.

Gradually I moved away from my teaching role in the local college. This was a time when the resurgence of community development in Ireland began in earnest. Many of us felt that inclusion, diversity and equality could be the essential basis for changing Ireland, especially for women. One thing

I knew intimately was how women's vulnerability could be a block to finding a path through. While I almost certainly had the advantage of growing up in a safe and loving home with enough to eat, changing things for the better was something I wanted deep in my bones. I knew what it was like to be uncared-for and forgotten.

In the 1990s I moved into working in community support. Early on, my role was to identify where there was a need for injections of EU funding that would level up some of the poorest communities in the country. The next step was to support these communities to access the funding and use it to develop their communities. This funding would eventually facilitate the growth of local projects to build an improved quality of life for many small and marginalised towns and villages all over Ireland.

We worked hard together to ensure that the resources went as close as possible to where the need was. Some groups чат8

wanted adult education as so many of their people had been forced to leave school early. Some needed childcare so that women could access training or go back to work. Others had older populations that needed services or some place to gather and maintain social contact. The idea was that there would be no 'one size fits all' approach.

Driving around the country I would often find myself in completely new territory. I got to know particular corners on the routes I took. The bend in the road out to Tullow where snowdrops appeared in their hundreds, the field in Carlow with a row of mature trees lined up across it, the slopes of Slieve na mBan like a woman at rest as I crossed Tipperary, the lush river crossing from Passage East to Ballyhack.

I was often told, 'This will never work here.' It was a challenging job at times as people were often hurt and bewildered by their previous brushes with the system. I sometimes felt like the meat in the sandwich between the worst of the bureaucracy and how change could be brought about by getting a handle on it.

Over those years we all lived through this 'quiet revolution'. Women, traditionally the backbone of daily life, began to move into the bigger arenas of decision making and many of the new jobs that were created locally.

Community work, caring, teaching and childcare all became paid work options for women during those years and their work was recognised as crucial in the economy. Women pushed their way onto boards of local development groups and brought their knowledge and understanding there.

Women began setting the agendas for social change and getting involved in politics. We may still be at the beginning of this work, but there is now an infrastructure and a core of experienced and vocal women to keep it moving.

Over the years, with many women leading the way, other excluded communities came in from the margins. Men also began to gravitate towards this new way of working collaboratively and many of them put their shoulders to the wheel. My Right-Hand Man did more than his share, setting up a network of support for vulnerable men and figuring out how men could also have better lives.

While the history of the movements for change in Ireland are often centred on what happened in Dublin, it's important to recognise that all over Ireland, where perhaps the changes were more urgent, change came mainly through this work by women. So many inspirational women who shared this small space in the tapestry of change.

But more than anything, our small group of rural women were in the thick of it and in it together.

COMPASSION

Life had dealt our dad some serious challenges, but gradually over time he was more able to show his soft side. If there was one thing I learned from him over the years it was his humility and compassion for other people who were suffering too. 'The poor divil,' he would say about some friend who had hit hard times.

He would tut-tut at discrimination or unfairness. He worked hard and also found time to be active in his union. He was kind and full of joy with young people who came to the house. His voice would drop to a soft tone. Or he would giggle like a boy. If anyone in the house was ill, Dad would find something to calm the fever or soothe the throat. Hot whiskey was always a favourite, and he liked nothing better than to cook something delicious or bring home a pocket full of toffees. Years later when I needed to put myself in the shoes of others, I remembered his compassion.

Once when delivering part of a training course to a group of women managers, I was trying to explore with them the different styles of leadership in organisations. So I put out a question to the group about how they might describe their own management style.

The contributions varied from an empowering management style to a structured leader. Then one woman, the manager of a community-based women's project, piped up, 'I'd call mine the Mammy style of management,' she said. This brilliant naming of something rarely mentioned made us all laugh and, whether we were mothers or not, we all had mothers of our own and could identify with the truth of it.

At the heart of it, managing and leading is pure compassion.

THE CAILLEACH

If you go back far enough to Irish myths and folklore, there are tales of powerful women, with moral authority, who own land, are healers, storytellers, weavers of the tapestry of life: Banba, the Banshee, Brigid, Clíodhna, Gráinne, Maeve.

Far from being the quiet princesses of faery tales that were told to us as children, these are powerful and complex goddesses, queens and saints. There is one complex female character from these myths, the Cailleach, the old woman, who embodies a big picture of female energy that is both colourful and dark. Just over the fields there, at the Hill of the Hag, the Cailleach is written into the landscape.

The Cailleach, the old hag, or the wise old woman, is most often depicted as having great powers to give and also to take away. At Bealtaine she is the midwife holding all the knowledge of birth and at Samhain she is the guide of the dying

and the dead. The Cailleach is attuned to the natural cycles of the seasons and her path is more of a spiral and less of a straight line. She is fierce, and if she gets out on the wrong side of the bed, beware!

The wise old woman has no need to slay the dragon or to develop a super powerful ego. She uses her powers to care, to create and to learn. She weaves her path through mythical tapestries, circles and spirals, the cycles of life, births and deaths, spiralling out and back in a whole series of lifespans. As I get older I begin to let her in – an old, wrinkled, crabby, wise and creative being.

On my walks I begin to imagine that the Inner Child and the Cailleach are binding together. That we are all a little part of this complex web of life, equal with the soil, the animals, the entire ecosystem. We are all Nature and she is us.

I lie on the beach in the autumn sun, listening to the waves crashing on the shore, and feel her power. I look up into the canopy of the forest and see her light filtering down through the leaves. I stare into the starlit sky and imagine her spinning in infinity. It is this Mother Earth, the macrocosm, the bigger picture, this wandering star amidst the cosmos that softly reveals the beauty of the everyday turning of the year.

Gradually my Inner Child allows the wise old Cailleach a bit more space and acceptance. Now when I look in the mirror, I see both.

SAMHAIN

On a Halloween night when a group of us women are celebrating the feast of Samhain, witches, ghouls and ghosts are centre stage as the veil is thin between worlds. We will light a fire in the forest and sip birch-leaf whisky from shot glasses. The children will roam the back roads and lanes disguised as their favourite characters or simply dressed in old clothes, hats and their parents' boots. Later they will play games dunking for apples or will eat too much colcannon just to see if they can win the ring (marriage) or the bean (wealth).

I remember Halloween in our Nanan's kitchen. Our Grand Aunt Nora was given the role of chief witch and at some point during the tea of nuts, barmbrack, (báirín breac, meaning 'speckled loaf') and apples, she would appear silently at the window in a ghoulish mask.

Once, me being me, I screamed out her name when she appeared. As disguise was everything to the adults, they were horrified by my big reveal. It was very important on

Halloween not to be recognised. This one night in the year, was for dressing up and sauntering around anywhere and everywhere as if you owned the place. Houses with long driveways or with quiet occupants would be top targets for visits. In those days we used to chant 'Help the Halloween Party' and be given sweets, nuts or more apples for our trouble in merely turning up with an old coat and cap on. But don't get recognised.

The dark had a huge attraction for us. Scared and clinging on to each other, we would secretly hope for a good fright as we rambled from house to house. Death, while not fully understood by us as children, was everywhere on the night of Samhain.

This year, out in the forest on a chilly autumn evening, the fire in the darkness is all ours. We older women, hags, crones have not fully forgotten how we forged our own path to get here. Tonight we are reminded again of that ancient rite; gathering, celebrating, rising up in our own way at the foot of the Hill of the Hag.

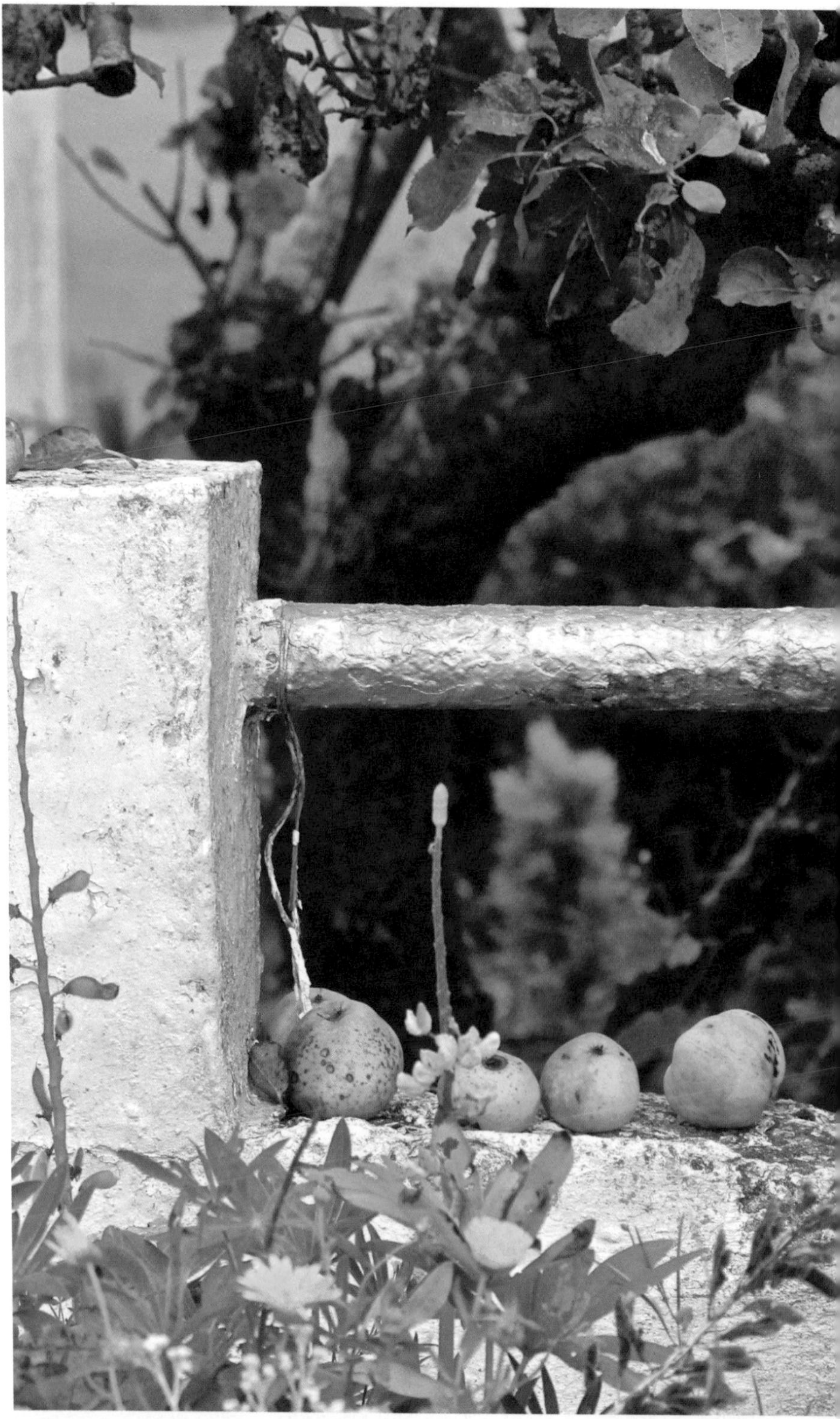

Chapter 12

Ripening

APPLES

Sometimes, for all kinds of reasons, life can be mysterious, unfathomable and dark with shadows. The beauty we find on any ramble in nature, in any familiar wrinkly old face, in the expression of flow through art can take us out of the gloomy into the exquisite.

The light fractures in the sway of golden leaves as I walk down the by now muddy lane. Potholes are filled with puddles reflecting the dancing leaves above. My neighbour has left apple cores and orange peels on her compost heap, much to the birds' delight. On the walls in the yard she has lined up apples that will later be fed to the horses up on the hilly field.

In a lockdown mood in autumn I photographed an apple. It began as a perfect organic red fruit in all its glory. Over weeks while it was in decline the entire apple shrank and wrinkled up in front of my eyes. Holding this apple in my own hands, the apple and I were ageing in unison.

I took to photographing apples in decline and my own skin wrinkling with the use of almost seven decades. The more the apple dried up and disappeared, the more I wondered about my own demise. There was essentially no difference between any kind of organic matter at the end of our days. We bloom, we fruit, we fade and we return to the earth.

And that is that. Autumn is the season of letting go, and there is comfort in that if we can allow ourselves to do it.

It was the neurologist, psychiatrist and Holocaust survivor Victor E Frankl who said, 'Yes to life, in spite of everything'. Those of us privileged to live the mystery of the slower ripening as we age say yes to our lives over and over again in spite of the ending that is inevitable.

GENERATIONS

As I held the crinkling apple in the palm of my hand, I wondered whether it had any awareness of itself as a seed, a fruit, a species, or even the life-giving earth itself. It's something I wonder about the ageing process in myself too. Growing older throws up a new question, how will I understand and manage my ending?

My hunches about death are not very well developed, but I have some. When I look back thousands of years to the people who walked these tracks and trails before me, I know that somewhere amongst them, some woman birthed

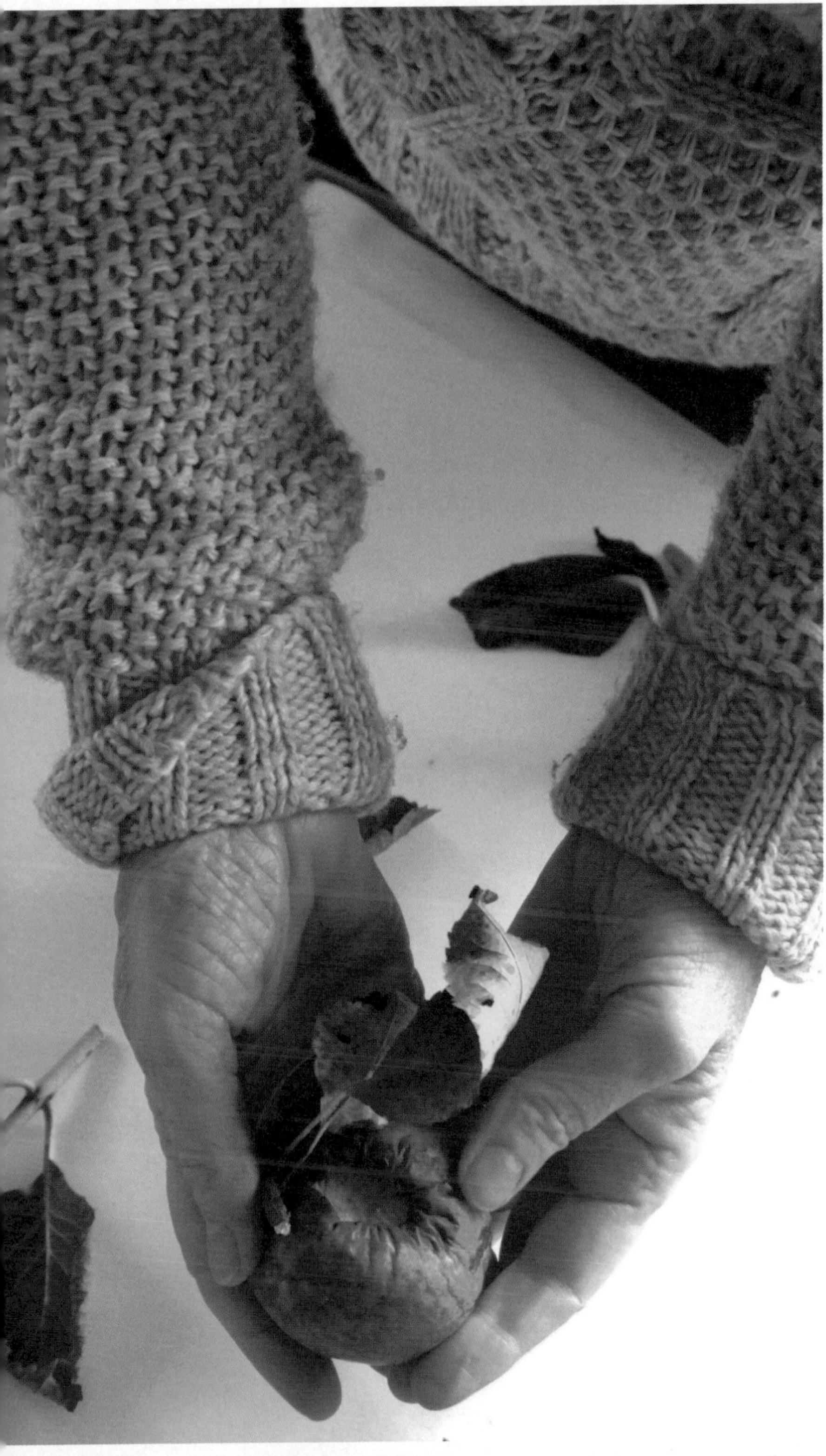

someone, who then birthed someone else who is possibly one of my ancestors. I will never know their names or their big questions, but somehow I got here because they survived and thrived.

The archaeologists of the future might just find my couple of acres with a ruined house in the centre of an overgrown forest. As they excavate, they could find bone samples from me and my family. They might find my art and wonder what drove this human to paint squiggles on found pieces of paper? Maybe they will wonder why I was so fond of eggs, and lived on omelettes and beetroot pickle?

I often think, as I chat to the robins or photograph hares, that I have lived with them for generations of their kind. And yet, each robin looks the same as its ancestors did. They even have the same little quirks and a taste for worms or black ants. Hares, for their part, like to take naps in the middle of the day. They graze on shoots and leaves only taking the sweetest and the newest. While I am getting to know one individual overall, they are continuing to thrive through the generations, not as individuals, but as a species.

Perhaps getting older leads us all to become just that, members of the human species. Just another example. But in my case, one that eats a lot of eggs.

THE OLD CHAIR

There's an old chair in the garden that is returning to nature in its own slow way. Its demise began with rusting legs and

general wonkiness, but it was still functioning as a chair for a while.

I had a great fondness for its shape and design so I ignored the fact that it was eventually useless for sitting on. Like a lot of old things, as it sank into the ground it grew more beautiful in my eyes. The Japanese call this phenomenon *wabi sabi*; the beauty of impermanence and imperfection.

Wabi sabi echoes through the landscape in Ireland. Crumbling remains of the past: old sheds and cottages, disused and abandoned for new bungalows and barns; stone walls built by the hands of ancestors and replaced by electric fencing and wire; an old barrel fixed into the gap in a ditch, rusting away for generations. Our eyes when attuned to the beauty of the imperfect can look more deeply into these rural remnants of the past. With a slight change of perspective, we can look closer to see how their ageing surfaces tell us different stories from the landscape.

Over time mosses grew on the wooden seat and back of the chair, and then over more time the most wonderful frilly lichens appeared.

This chair could have been dumped on the scrap heap or burnt on a fire. But this way, its slow ageing can become a home for other species, a thing of beauty and a reminder of old times.

ECOLOGICAL ENDINGS

We are squeamish about death, not just in the sadness we feel, but in our lack of imaginative thinking about it. Death sometimes gets layered over with shame and silence, which is far more damaging to loved ones than openness and remembrance. Somehow in autumn we are reminded of the beauty of leaves falling and the wonder of golden light on ripening berries. The beauty of returning to the earth.

Walking in this turning time of autumn, I imagine a similar ecological solution to my own death and the beginnings of some fresh thinking about our burial traditions. Not to put too fine a point on it and without in any way meaning to be disrespectful, there is a toxicity to being laden with chemical embalming fluids then buried in a graveyard which, although sometimes beautiful and comforting, must surely be one of the most poisoned gardens in the world.

Ecological burials and the cultivation of a neutralising fungus that will turn us and our mercury fillings into organic compost is an acceptance and responsibility even in

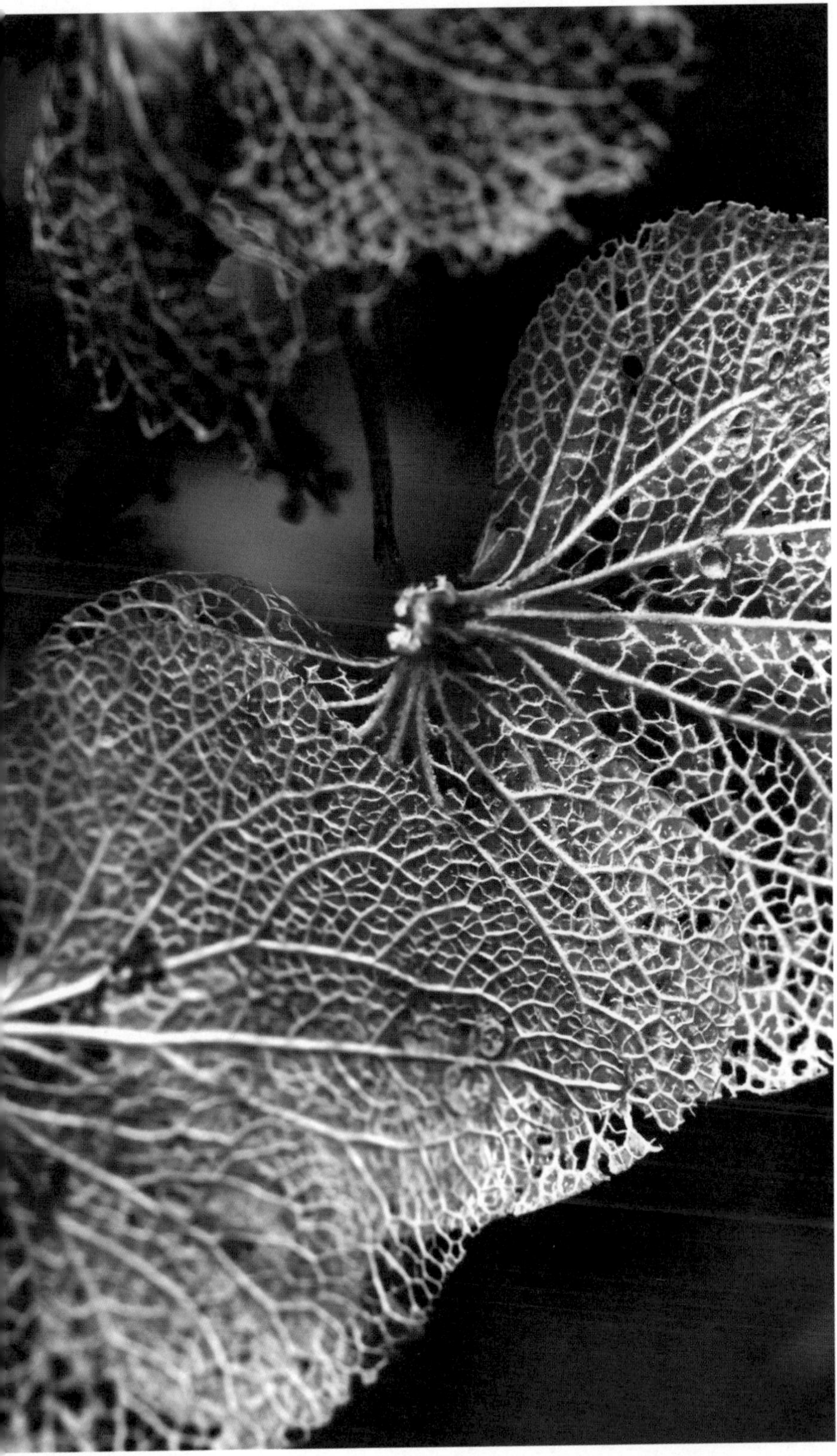

death and about minimising our footprint on our fragile ecosystem. While we are here, let's enjoy it, but when we die, let's do it with more imagination, and some connection with the earth and future generations that can benefit from our thoughtfulness.

FAMILY

As I ripen into old age, the younger generations, my sons, their friends, nieces and nephews, grandnieces and nephews, children of friends bloom into a different phase of life. As we gather in the luscious fruit of autumn, I remember when they were all small and the days were drawing in.

In those days I lived with my Right-Hand Man and the three boys in an old stone cottage. It might have been tumbling down around us, but we were cosy there, baking scones and making a big creative experiment out of the whole place. Maybe it was me who benefited most?

Each of our children brought the gifts of magical small people with ideas and thoughts all of their own. Each one came into the world with a personality and a whole set of qualities unique to them. It took time to get to know each one and for each of them to find ways to live life on their own terms.

All those years of their youth the house was a menagerie of pet mice, gerbils, rabbits, dogs and cats. We even took trips in the van with the pets on board. Once a budgie was stolen from the van and held for ransom in the flats of inner-city

Dublin. When I parked the car outside a shop, one of the lads released the handbrake and went sailing past as I was paying for the milk. There were too many adventures to even mention. Looking back all I can feel is how lucky I have been to experience it all.

Even now, the younger generation remind me, as I spend precious time in their adult company, that no one on their deathbed ever said, I wish I had spent more time in the office. I am often bewildered by the intensity of the connection and the joy I feel in their presence. It's an instinctive love that burns bright. I wonder how hard it was for Addie to let go of it.

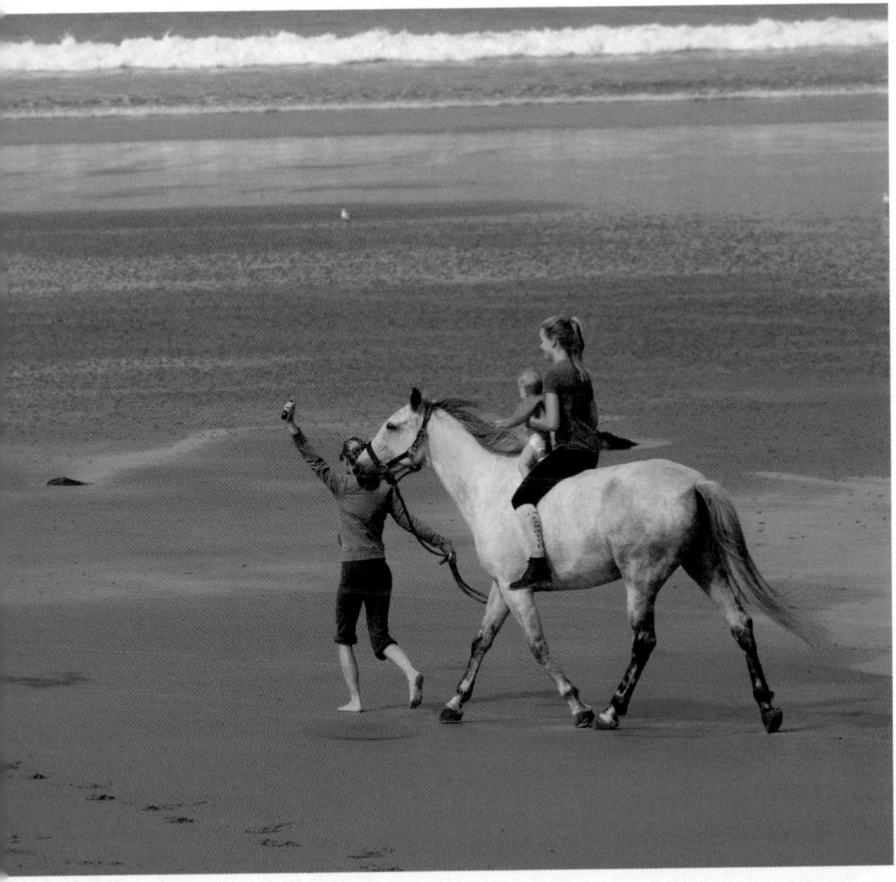

WINTER

Breathing space

Teachtaireacht Bhríd

(Oíche Nollag Ré Lán 2015)

Is beag comhluadair a chothaigh an oíche gheal

Do na h-imircigh aonaránacha a theith óna muintir

'S a threasnaigh an teorainn shléibhtiúil ina raibh

A gcroíthe siocaithe ag an oighear

Bhí an t-ádh leis an mbuachaill ón Afganastán

A chuimhnigh ar glaoch a chuir ar Naomh Bríd

An bhean a shiúl ar uisce na locha is a leag

Driseacha do phaisinéirí

Dúisíodh Bríd ó chodladh an Gheimhridh

Ag fothain Ghobnait i mBaile Mhúirne

Nuair a chuala sí olagón an ógánaigh n'fhéadadh sí ach a rá:

'Nach gcíonn tú an ghealach chéanna a chímse?'

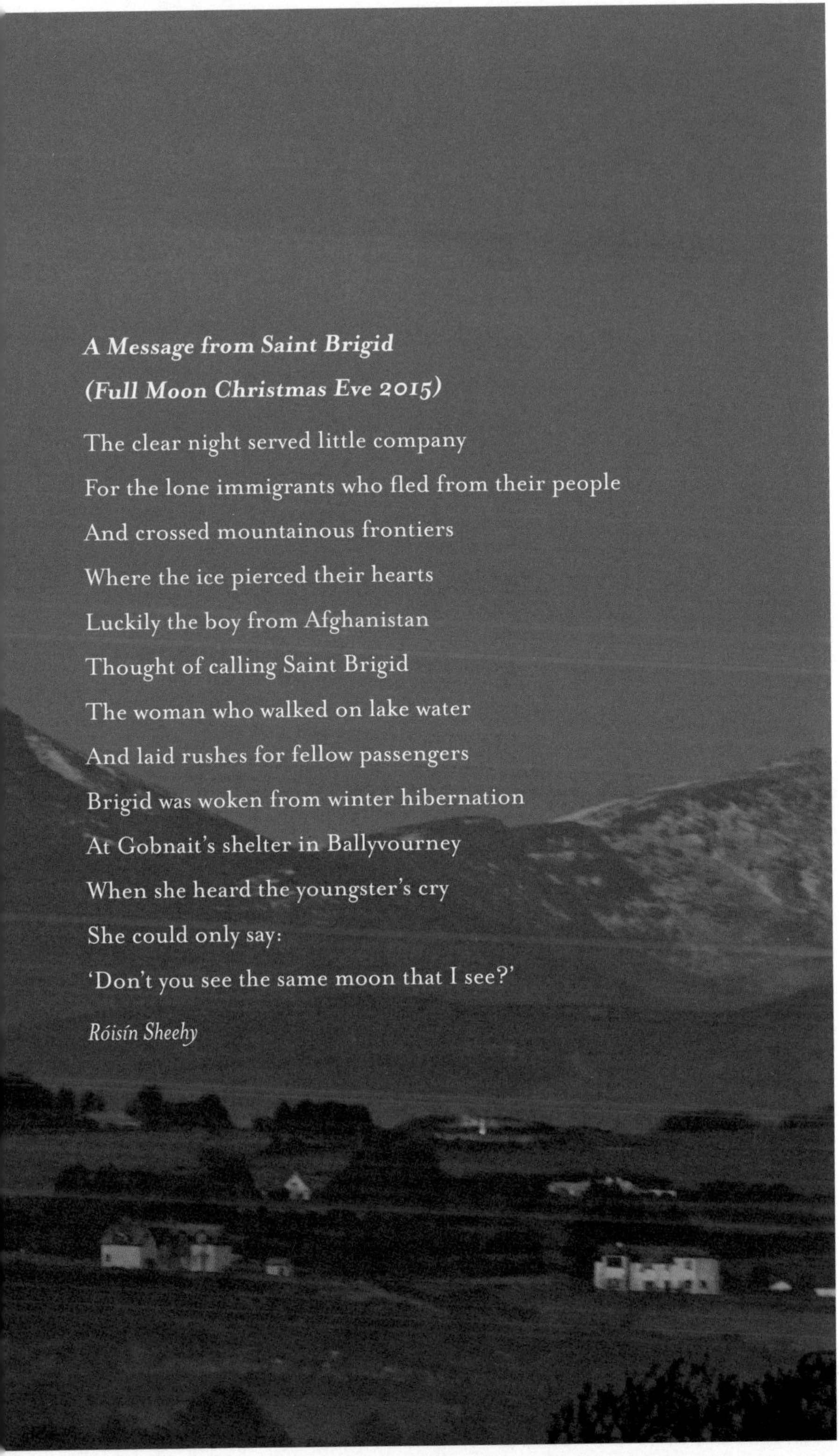

A Message from Saint Brigid

(Full Moon Christmas Eve 2015)

The clear night served little company
For the lone immigrants who fled from their people
And crossed mountainous frontiers
Where the ice pierced their hearts
Luckily the boy from Afghanistan
Thought of calling Saint Brigid
The woman who walked on lake water
And laid rushes for fellow passengers
Brigid was woken from winter hibernation
At Gobnait's shelter in Ballyvourney
When she heard the youngster's cry
She could only say:
'Don't you see the same moon that I see?'

Róisín Sheehy

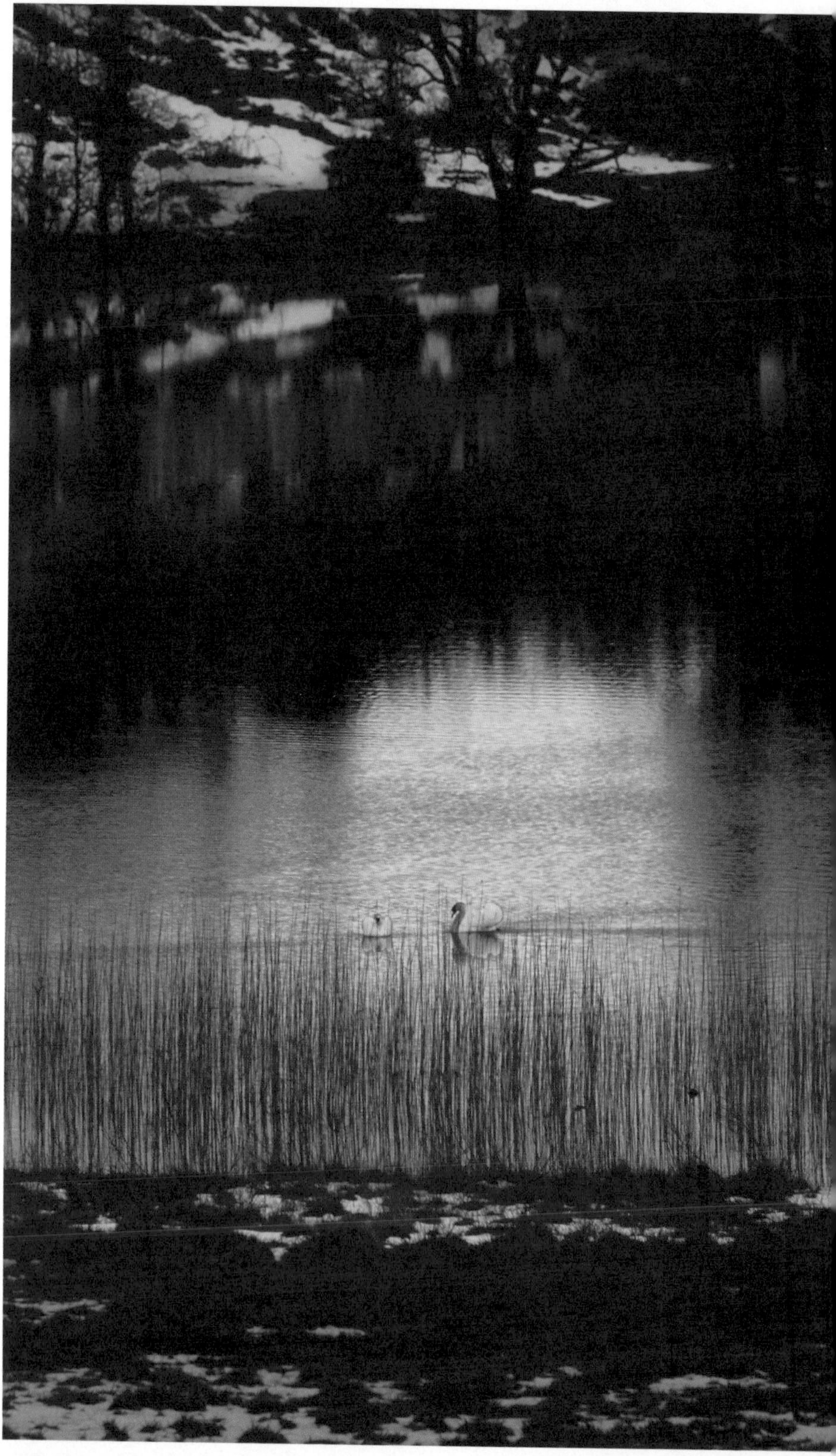

Chapter 13

Hibernation

WRAPPING UP

Maybe our ambivalence about winter was passed down through the generations: the fear of cold dark evenings and being cooped up inside. But winter is also a time for the pleasure of laying low. As we huddle and build fires, the winter months become a creative hibernation of sorts. Thankfully one of the great revelations through the magic of photography is the exquisite beauty of winter, especially the still and icy mornings of the first frosts.

As the dawn breaks on a dark morning, very little stirs. The sun creeps up over the hill to the east and seeing the cool diagonal beams of light entices me to grab the camera, wrap up and venture out before it is quite daylight. Those first beams of light will catch the still-frozen dew on leaves and branches and when I turn the lens into the dawn it will capture the icy fragments of tiny rainbows and sunbeams.

In every way, winter light is a joy. Summer light, for all its dazzling showiness, lacks the depth of winter contrasts; how the dark outline of trees, with their massive skeletons exposed, allow crows to gather in full view. These trees, like huge beings, normally disguised by heavy layers of leaves, display their fractal shapes, throwing long shadows across the land.

Animals are slower to emerge on these winter mornings. As the cold weather sets in, birds wait anxiously for the breakfast spread of sunflower hearts and scraps and there are more of them waiting each day.

All through the winter months, south-westerly storms threaten from the Atlantic. Sometimes it's best to simply face the music, get booted up and go out, head down, into the wind. But there are far more occasions that on these windy days, like any hibernating hedgehog, I stick my snout out into the wind and retreat back inside. The pet days for me are when it snows and we wake up in a silent, soft world of an undulating whiteout.

Snow events, although rare here, usually cut us off from the main road. The big snow of 2010 saw the lake freeze over. An elderly man walked down there to see it and said there hadn't been a freeze like it since 1963 — that winter when my sister Grace and I got our first corduroy pants and skated on a frozen pond in our wellies.

More recently in a storm, huge drifts of snow filled the lanes, and the ditches all but disappeared. When the snow 'sticks' in Ireland and our landscape becomes a Christmas card, we are all children again lapping up every small icy moment of it.

Winter days here often end with dramatic sunsets over the lake that illuminate the kitchen as we make dinner. On the winter solstice, when the daylight hours are shortest, you can't help but reflect on the beauty and the mystery of it all. These fiery evening skies and the western light fill the land with a few moments of warmth. Then suddenly all is cool and dark.

THE ROBIN

In early winter, the robin shows up on more than the Christmas cards beginning to appear in the shops. Robins have a habit of following what they obviously define as intruders in

their territory. When many other birds are silent, the robin's song is clearer and brighter in winter. At first, on winter walks I found this quite unsettling. Why did the robin appear at the same spot every day, puff himself up and bounce up and down on his thin legs as if to warn me away?

I would stop to observe this performance in detail in my neighbour's farmyard as I walked through to follow the track to the abandoned reservoir. The folk tale about the robin making an appearance around the death of someone wasn't lost on me. Robins in Irish folklore are often messengers from the spirit world. My robin, unusual amongst small birds, would stand his ground and look straight back confidently.

These plucky little birds are more relaxed around humans than other species and have probably learned that we will feed them. A robin companion will follow a gardener too, seemingly delighted by the production of a spade or a fork. A worm will provide a substantial meal for a robin and if it means being more visible, no problem. There have now been generations of them in our garden, but each new offspring will have similar characteristics so that over time it seems that the very same robin has always been present.

A robin stands her ground as an individual rather than as part of a group. Finches will always come in groups and a 'charm of goldfinches' is common around here. But the robin comes alone, especially in winter; stands on the perch of a rock or comes to the window to remind us that she is there and that we are a source of sustenance.

Retreat

In Sweden, where my sister Grace now lives, bright images of children skiing and cooking sausages out in the snow are fantasy winter scenes to us. In Ireland grey days and the damp westerly airflow are more likely on Christmas Day than icy mornings. But even grey light has its place in a photographer's repertoire. There are deep blue-grey skies with squinting sunlight and there are soppy pale-grey days when the light is so diffused there are no shadows, just murky sameness. Even then, as long as there is no wind, grey is perfect for enhancing small details.

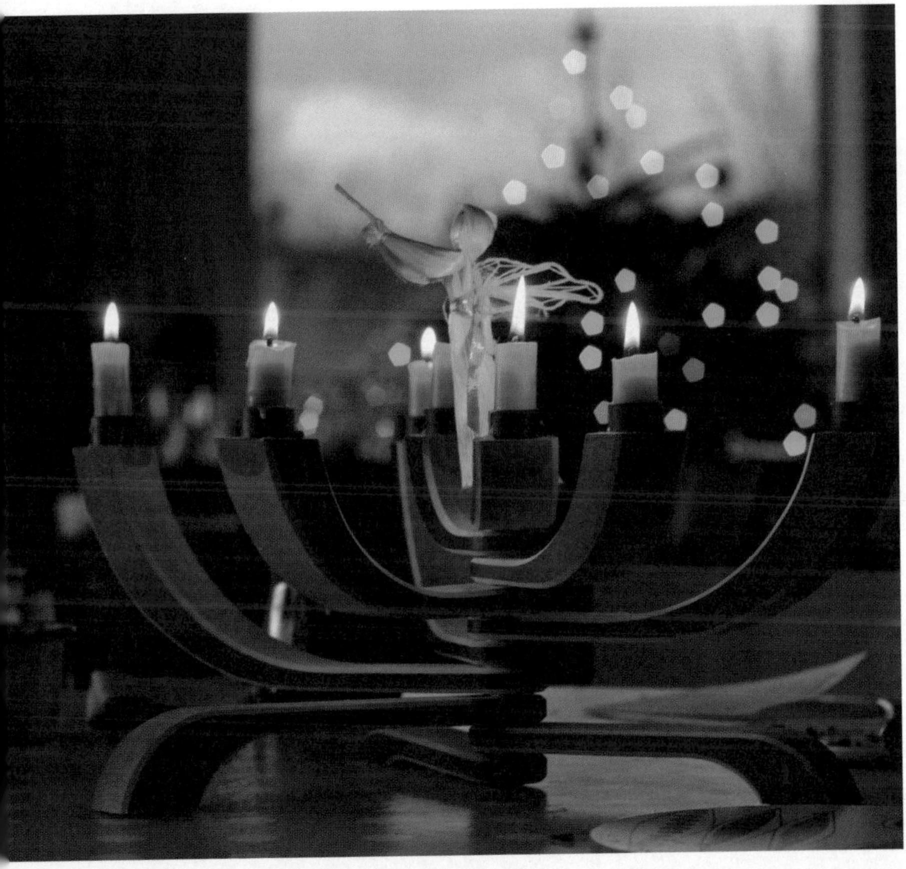

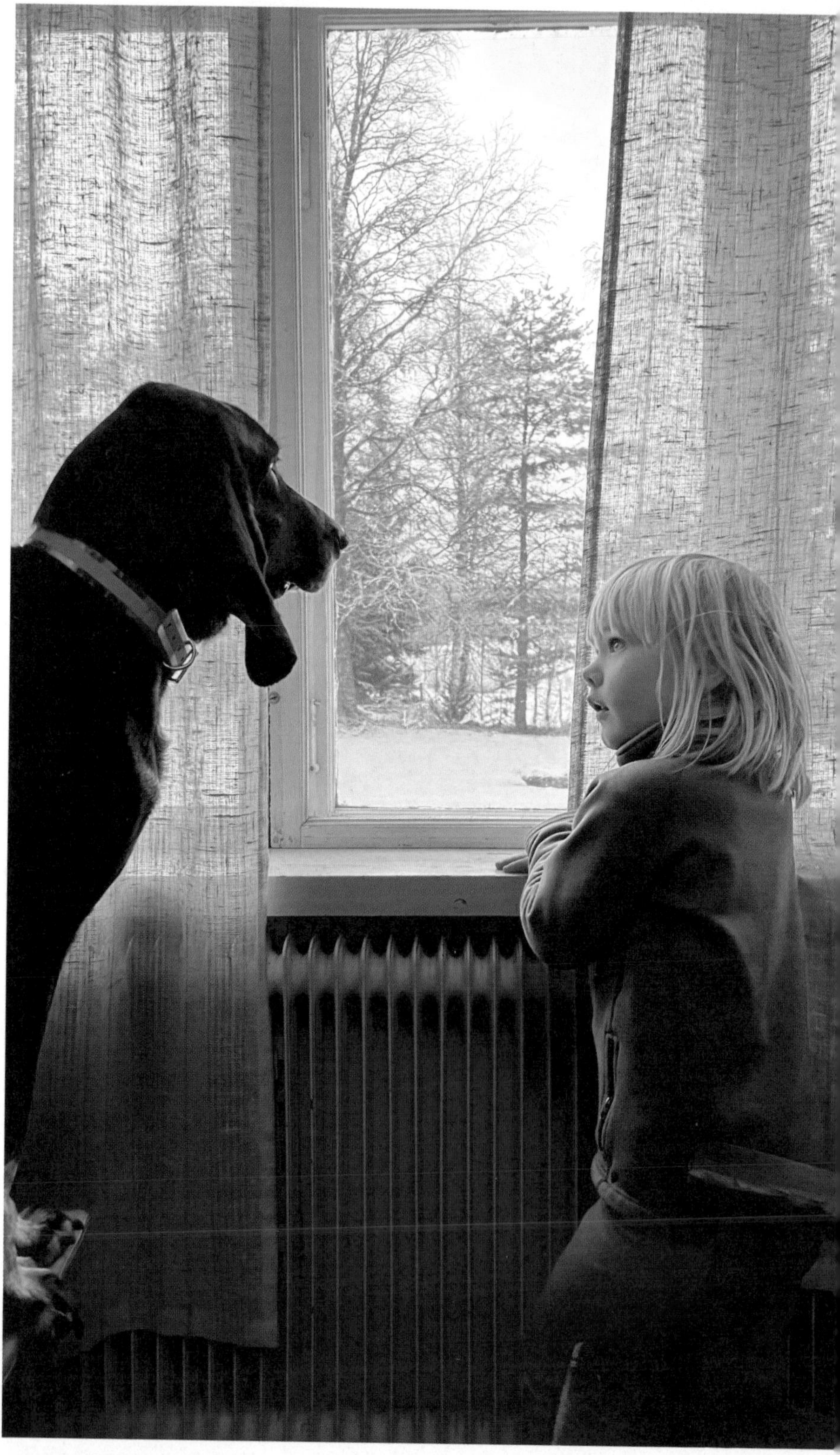

In the depths of winter, Irish people ease themselves into a retreat, gather around a roaring fire or light candles to ward off the gloom. Christmas or any version of the traditional mid-winter festival is a feast of flickering light and an embrace of family. We batten down the hatches and make the most of the relaxation. There are feasts of rich food, warm drinks of sloe gin or celebratory ones with bubbles. We stay warm, play scrabble and watch old movies on TV.

In our family, our youngest son brings dress-up themed outfits and accessories for our annual Christmas snap. These pictures require everyone's best acting, production and photographic skills as well as an element of risk. It could be us posing as undercover agents in furry hats and military coats, or as stand-ins for Rip Van Winkle treading up to bed with lit candles.

On the first Christmas Day of the pandemic we made fires outside under the stars and danced in the icy air – a full-on celebration of survival and the turning of the year. But inside, cosiness supports the soul in a time of interior living and interior life. Hunkering down is its own kind of solace.

CHRISTMAS

Christmastime has that way of leading us back to our own childhood memories, and our first Christmas without Addie is etched in mine. Neighbours and relatives did everything they could to help Dad cope with being a lone parent to four girls under nine.

Meanwhile, aunties took over. My almost-toothless grand aunt, who we adored, was going to make tam-o'-shanters for Christmas. The mystery of this gift would keep me up at night wondering what they were. To me, they sounded like bad news. A kind of hat, I was told.

Another auntie took measurements because she was going to join in the fun and sew us capes for Christmas Day. Yes, identical capes, one for each of us, to match the tam-o'-shanters. 'The Beatles have capes,' she enthused! 'Didn't you see them on that record of "Help!"' I checked it out. Yes, those black capes looked good on The Beatles. Maybe a tam-o'-shanter was like what John Lennon was wearing? I told the little ones, 'We are going to be just like The Beatles.' They peered at the one photo we had on that small EP. Then we played 'Help!' all day, dancing around and imagining our new Christmas-Day outfits.

Dad wanted to take us to see Santa before Christmas and, as a special treat, we were going to see *Snow White*. This was a Walt Disney update of a cartoon Dad had seen as a child. He said we would love it. Feeling way too grown up for any of it, I was peeved, but as with everything else we four girls moved as one. So off we all went.

Snow White was a terrifying film. There was an awful old witch in it and whenever she appeared our youngest would insist on going to the toilet. 'Take your sister to the Ladies,' I would be told. With a wistful sigh and my eyes glued to the screen, I would be dragged in there so she could dilly dally as long as possible so as not to have to face the terror.

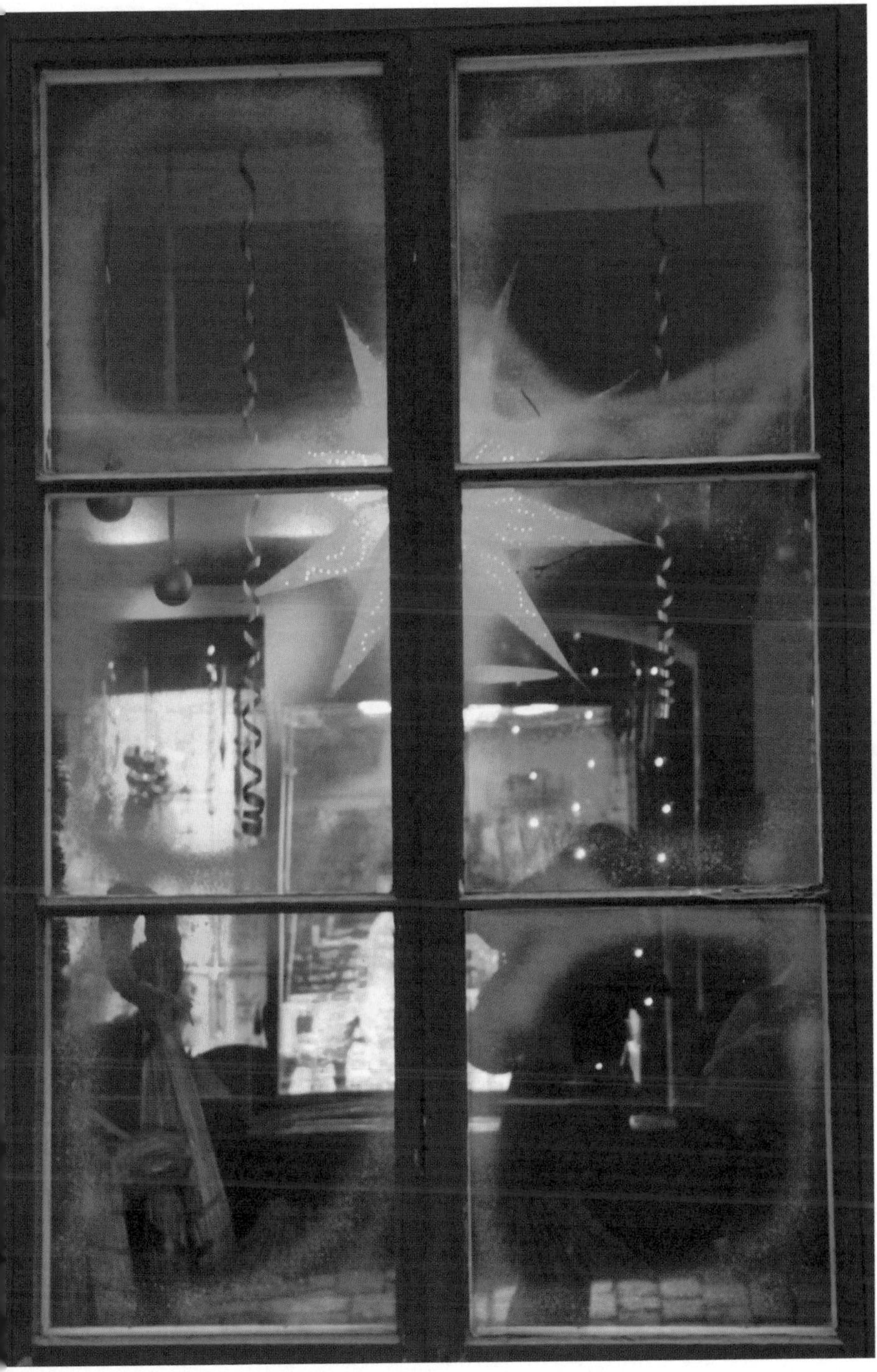

'Don't like that old witch,' she would wail. We were missing the film. As usual there I was, entertaining young ones in the toilets or the sweet shop whenever they were scared or bored. When I eventually got back in my seat, I glared at Dad and said, 'It's not fair.' He gave me a pleading look.

Christmas week was hectic and we were all sky high as rockets. We spent a lot of time preparing a Christmas Show that would feature the four of us singing 'Help!' in our new capes and hats. I had it all figured out. The 'good room' was the stage. The sliding doors between the back room and the good room would be the curtains. Then there was the bendy lamp that could be used as a spotlight onto our stage.

The aunties and our granny would be spending Christmas with us. We dropped endless hints to everyone and anyone about dolls that could walk and talk and two-wheeler bikes. I imagined Christmas morning over and over. I couldn't sleep for fantasising about bikes!

Christmas morning came. The capes were unwrapped first. They were blue, 'powder blue' the aunties informed us. The enormous tam-o'-shanters were cream-coloured woolly yokes. I stared at the outfits and tried not to think of John Lennon too much. Dad didn't help matters by saying he would be mortified walking up the aisle at the Christmas Mass with the four of us looking like the Artane Boys Band.

The aunties gave him a filthy look.

The little ones seemed thrilled. The aunties dressed them up and were delighted at how posh they looked. This was my living nightmare. At the age of ten, all I wanted was to be treated as a 'grown up'. Here they were making out I was just another little kid. To make matters even worse, I had to join in and wear the awful matching powder-blue capes or risk disappointing everyone. I looked like rubbish.

'Off we go,' said Dad. 'The rest of the presents can be opened after Mass.' This was the Christmas tradition. We certainly turned heads that Christmas morning when we turned up at the church in a procession of powder blue. I prayed hard for a better day ahead. I still had all my hopes pinned on a two-wheeler bike. I said all the prayers and sang all the hymns I could to make it happen.

Once home, we rushed in to the Christmas tree. Sadly it was an artificial one, which looked nothing like a proper tree. I judged that Dad had failed this test too, like so many others. And now for the final test. His presents to us.

Cowboy suits and guns.

My gun shot darts with a sucky end for firing at windows. I shot my sister in the middle of the forehead with it. The dart stuck and wobbled for a second or two before her crying started. She had a ping-pong gun, but try as she might she couldn't get me back with it. I very brazenly called out that didn't hurt whenever one sort of landed!

Although the cowboy suits were fun, Dad had proven yet again that he hadn't got a CLUE about GIRLS! What was wrong with him?!

Later, he got all upset about the turkey that he had won playing golf. It wouldn't cook properly as it was twenty-four pounds in weight and barely fitted into the oven. He broke out in a sweat and said, 'Christ Almighty' and 'the whole thing is a feckin' hames'. We did a disappearing act and went into the good room to rehearse our show, *Help!* Dressed in the four capes we knew the performance would go down very well that evening, but the curtain call for an encore required another strategy. We needed a boy. Luckily, the family next door had a boy of their own, so we borrowed him for our version of 'Seven little girls, sittin' in the back seat, kissin' and a-huggin with Fred'. Miming to yet another disc in Dad's collection.

The Show was a triumph. We were on fire!

Later Dad finally fell asleep in an armchair. Granny tried to teach us Rummy, but we ended up playing Snap all night as it was the only thing the younger kids could manage. She promised me quietly that she would play Rummy with me later, when the little ones were asleep.

At last I felt so grown up and special! Myself and the next sister were allowed to stay up after the TV finished, sit down with Granny and the aunties and play adult cards. When I tipped my cowboy hat to them and fired off a few darts, they laughed hysterically. But every so often they got a bit teary, took out their hankies and sniffled into them. When they got too sad, my sister cheered them up with her Calamity Jane act, standing up on the arm of a chair and shooting off her ping-pong gun at the ceiling.

Later, they tucked us into bed. The grand aunt mumbled our favourite ditty, 'Her foot slipped, down she fell and broke her alicabuzelam.' The aunties kissed us fondly and said, 'Night night, sleep tight and don't let the bugs bite.'

Dad appeared at the door. 'Goodnight, chickens,' he said and blew us kisses. I fell into a deep sleep dreaming of a million ways to get my hands on a two-wheeler bike. Maybe next year ...

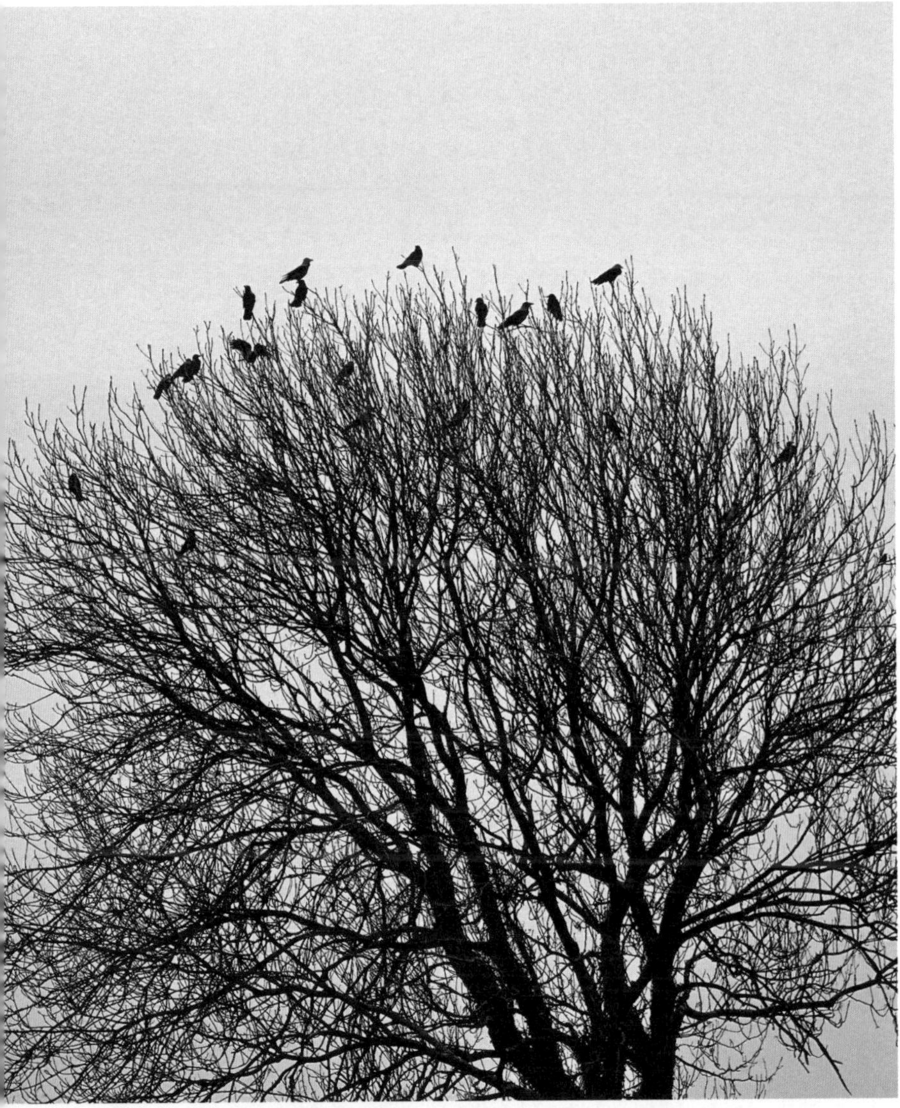

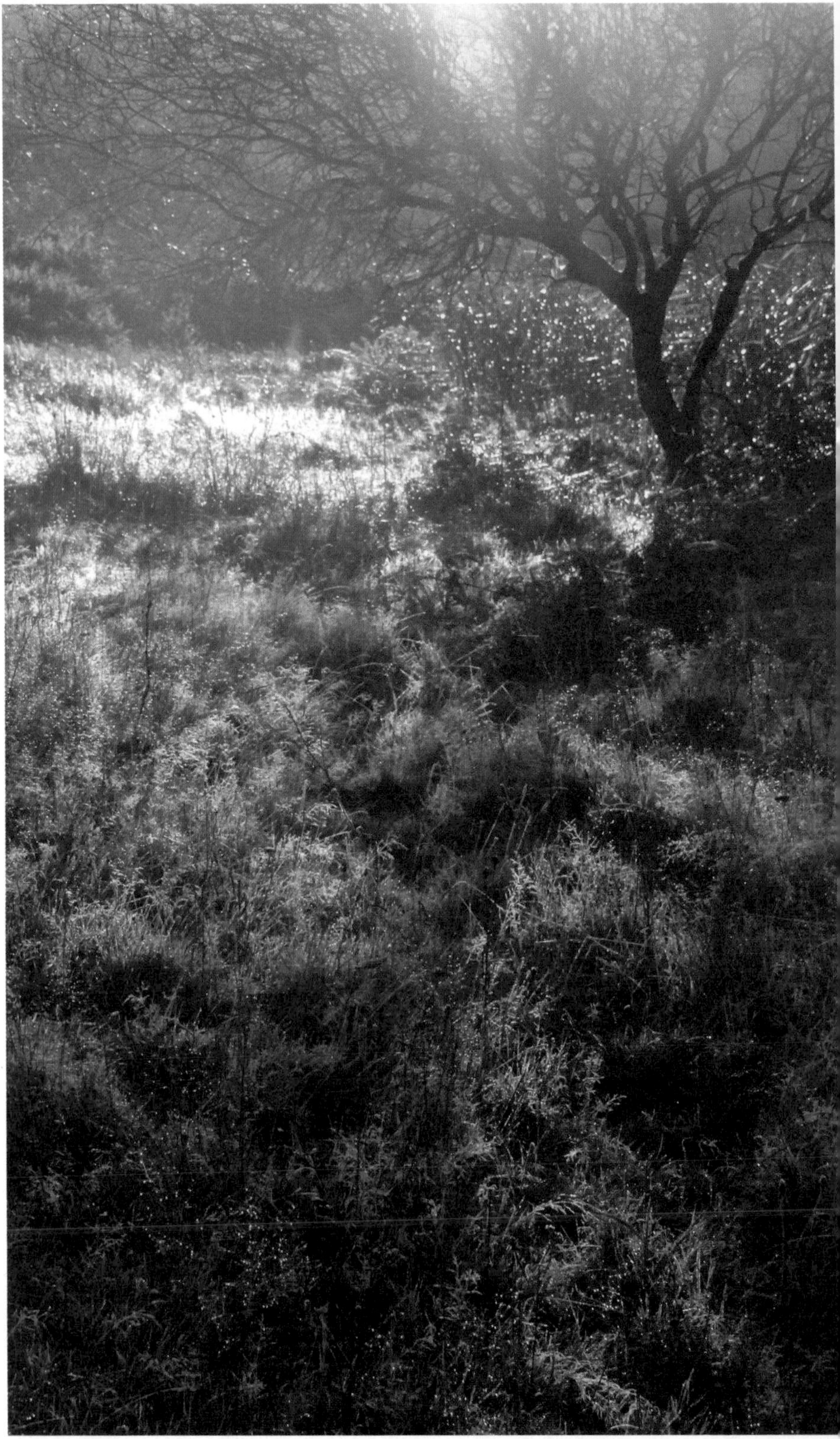

Chapter 14

Healing

WHERE THE VEIL IS THIN

What is most heightened when immersed in the natural world is the endless mystery of why and how we are here, which only deepens with age — in the winter of our lives. I am continually baffled by the scale of the universe, the wonder of the diversity on planet Earth, and how our ancestors paved the way for our survival. Perhaps the sparseness of winter allows a little more mystery to linger.

There are places where these mysteries are more intense — places of devotion or where the 'veil is thin'. In Ireland these places are associated with a permeable skin between the world of the living and the dead, the human and the mystical. These are places where generations of humans paused and prayed, where they pleaded or cried, where they celebrated births or commemorated their dead. You don't have to share a belief or a connection to a specific religion or culture to feel the balm of these places. It is in the land, the space and the light.

Mysteries are not only observed in traditional devotional places like the interiors of churches or dedicated buildings, sacred wells or ancient burial sites. There are also special places where humans have gathered or worked, where the physical world and the ethereal worlds are in harmony. Sometimes you can feel the energy of a mill, a barn or an artist's studio with a particular vibration.

Wherever we are in the world, we can tune into this unfathomable transcendence that can be seen or unseen. As I have a fairly fluid sense of what might or might not be, the freedom to explore and experience devotional spaces is something I treasure. The generosity of so many open doors and the sharing of these places around the world is a precious gift.

Not all so-called religious buildings strike this note. It is always interesting to compare churches, temples, grottos, sacred stones and gathering places for this enigmatic experience. There are random places where tears will come to your eyes, your heart will race or you will fall into a deep meditation. I remember seeing Sydney Harbour for the first time and welling up. Maybe an ancestral spirit is alive in that place, or maybe the beauty of the Bridge and the creative brilliance of the Opera House honour their place so that we are moved by the splendour of it? You can't always predict how a place will wash over you.

Lighted candles, images of saints or holy ones, incense,

fresh flowers, beads, gold, carvings, votives, the May Tree laden with flimsy offerings and desperate notes for help, which I used to find so spooky as a child — all the variety of small details can layer on atmosphere. Humans have never lost touch with the need to experience magic and mystery. The love of creeping into a shaded woodland or tiptoeing under a starlit sky.

In my own neck of the woods there is a beautiful graveyard overgrown with wildflowers. The simple act of not mowing or trimming has by chance created the most ethereal place of contemplation. The land sweeps down to a large natural harbour and the undulating swathes of daisies and buttercups are only interrupted by some very old headstones. Something or someone made it so and it moves us.

I can wallow in these hallowed places. As American poet Walt Whitman said, 'Re-examine all you have been told at school or church or in any book, and dismiss whatever insults your own soul.' Your soul knows what it loves and what feeds you, even if you don't. And your soul, if you are lucky, will know before you do what you need to dismiss. And all you have to do is pay attention.

Each of us is free to find our own source of solace and place. Some of us will be immersed in the exploration of mystery and beauty. Others will find a niche of belief or spiritual practice that will suit their soul and answer their questions. Our souls pick and choose from all kinds of sources to enrich our inner lives.

The beauty of the soul's meanderings is its ability to

combine the rational and the mythical. So it is no contra-
diction to explore the stories and the deeply held devotions
of our past as a species and at the very same time be open to
science and the need to validate the materiality of things.

<h1 align="center">QUESTIONS</h1>

The subject most prioritised for the first few years of my
schooling was religious instruction: learning your prayers,
studying the green catechism and singing hymns. We used
to make our First Holy Communion, a big initiation cer-
emony, at the age of six or seven, so the study for that was
fairly intense.

All of the Christian story was told to us as truth and fact,
so much so that it had a huge impact on my child's percep-
tion of the world. I became deeply devout during those
years, absorbing everything exactly as I was told. Just like the
faery stories of mirrors that could talk and animals that wore
clothes, angels that could fly and saints that could perform
miracles seemed real. Added to that was the complexity of
Catholic doctrine, which was excellent early training for
anyone seeking to become a barrister in later life! I prayed
energetically for all sorts of intentions and wore a scapular
made of rope around my waist as penance for the world.

That First Holy Communion, in the white dress and veil,
was the beginning of a conflict between the story of Chris-
tianity and my inner more feral nature. I think a lot of us
girls of that generation learned to hide ourselves under that

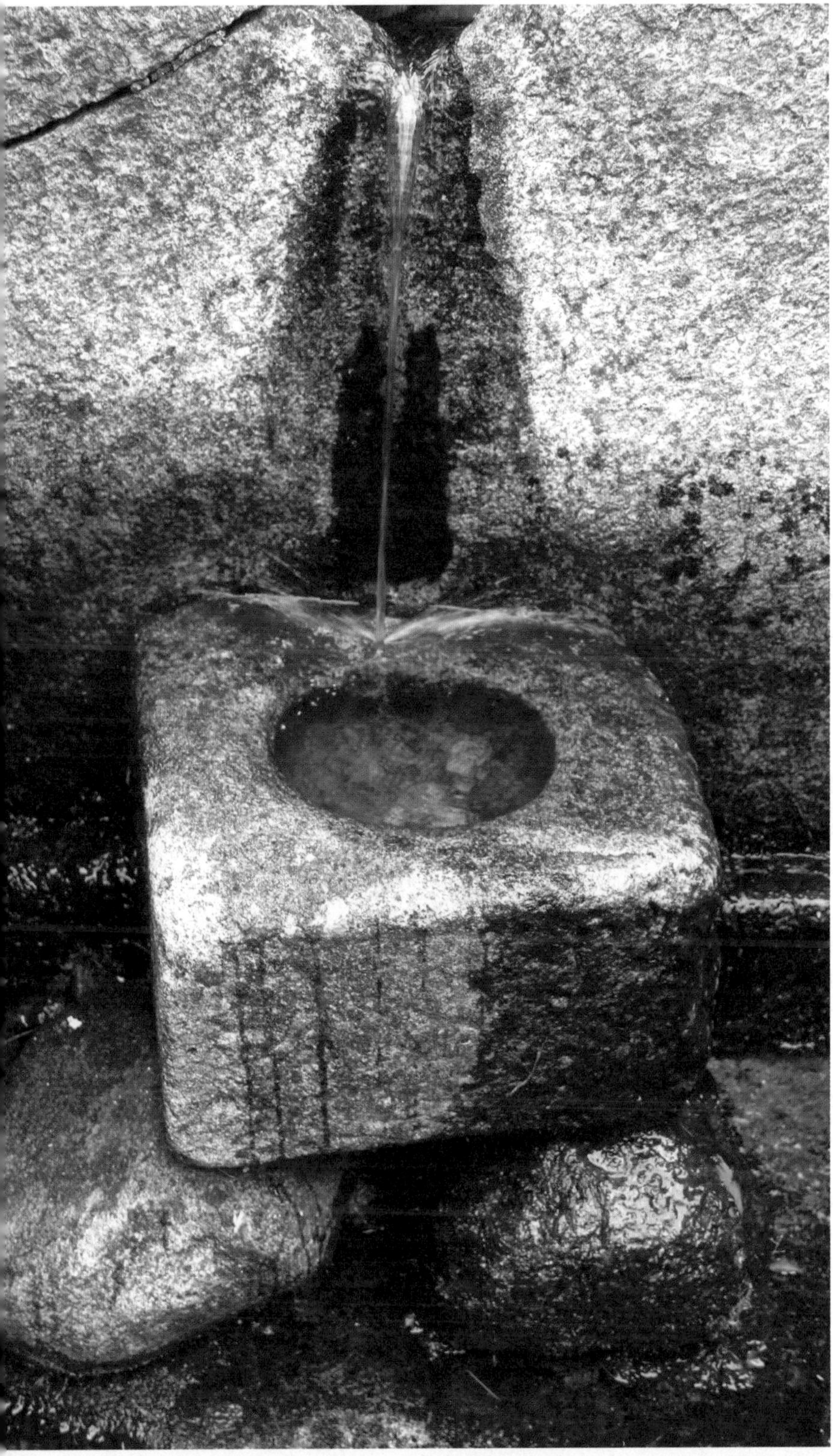

virginal white costume. I gradually became more quiet and contemplative, observing adults very closely, and wondering who and what to trust.

I was a good girl and Catholicism filled a space where my questions had been. For a while I was happy to lead my life of play and fun, and at the same time worship this triangular God family, with the Father, the Son and the Holy Spirit who was always pictured as a dove. The Mother of God, a martyr of sorts, wasn't a God herself. It was clear from her status and role what kind of future life would be mapped out for any Catholic girl — some kind of chaste, silent martyrdom.

Years later, we would all learn about the opportunity for oppression that this situation created for many children. I'm not sure how a group of four vulnerable girls like us with no mother and a frequently absent father escaped the abuse and torture meted out to many Irish children in that era. How did we manage to avoid it? It couldn't just have been luck.

If it wasn't luck, then the adults around us knew very well the dangers and protected us. If it was luck, then that came with the privilege of our inner resourcefulness that must have sent a strong, don't-mess-with-me message. That and our tight-knit closeness as sisters.

Trust is something you feel in your bones. Being a wounded child, just like any small animal, I always had a heightened sense of alertness to danger. While this has been a useful life skill, it can also add a layer of caution in perfectly safe situations and it takes longer for me to make up my mind about what's going on. This was all intuition as I was given no instruction in trust, except never to take sweets from a stranger.

Whatever gets you through the night

By the time I was fifteen, I had told Dad that I couldn't go to Confession any more as I had no sins. My father sent me to discuss this and all my favourite agnostic themes with the local parish priest. This came in the aftermath of a prolonged retreat at the church delivered by a 'singing priest', who had introduced a number of sexual topics that we had absolutely no previous knowledge or experience of. (He was later believed to have had a number of children and was far from leading a celibate life himself.)

Dad was continually bewildered by all my questions and had now washed his hands of the whole business. Again

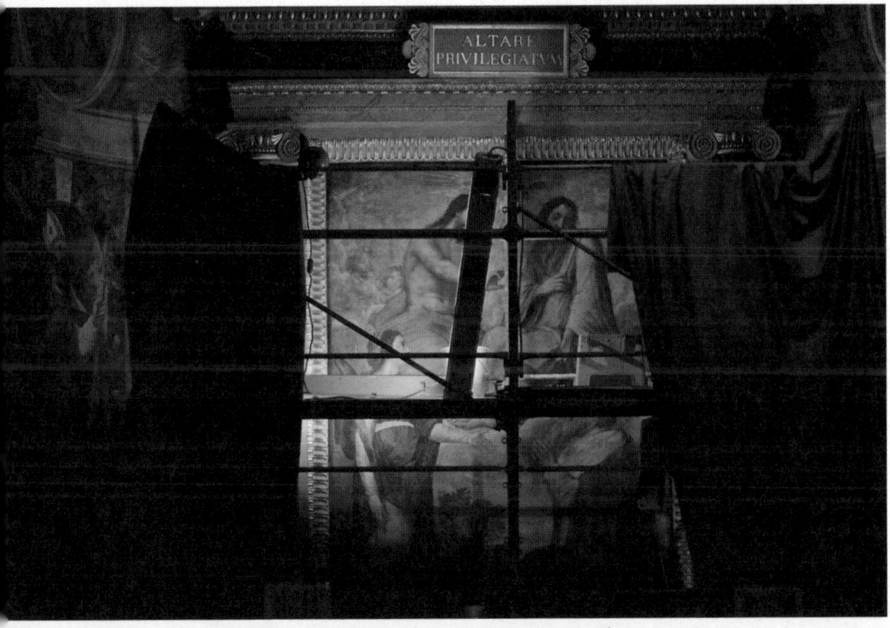
ALTARE
PRIVILEGIATVM

maybe I got lucky. The priest I was sent to gave me tea and biscuits and listened as I made my many points. He didn't argue back much, but did try to engage me about the question of Confession.

'Why do venial sins require regular Confession? I have no mortal sins at all, never having the chance to commit adultery or murder anyone,' I argued.

The priest listened to it all thoughtfully and after a while he told me to go home.

'What will I say to Dad?'

'Tell him I said that you are free not to come to Confession, but that I'd like you still to come to Mass.'

When I told Dad what the priest had said, he just shrugged his shoulders and finally released his hold on my freedom of thought. I felt sad if it had hurt him as he was a good person always trying to obey the Church teaching. Years later, he bemoaned his adherence to eating only fish on Fridays and suchlike when the Church decided to abolish some of the traditional practices he had grown up with.

'What was it all about?' he would say, bewildered.

I know now that like so many people of that generation he lived in fear of stepping outside what he had been taught. It was the same with his safe job of forty years, although in his particular situation it would have been impossible to take any risks. My sprawling, varied working life completely baffled him.

It seemed that unlike Dad, I had an uncanny ability to tolerate open questions and uncertainty. In the end the not knowing was easier for me to grasp than the dogma of Catholicism. We thrive on stories especially when they offer hope. Isn't it a triumph of the human imagination that we create stories about eternity when the only thing that is certain is our inevitable demise? People make the best of whatever gets them through the night and there is a warm blanket of solace for many in that.

SOLACE

I didn't find solace in the Christian story, but in love and being immersed in the beauty of our precious time here in the world. Being close to Mother Earth and feeling the wonder that I first felt as a small child allowed a deeper sense of belonging to it all.

The search for solace didn't stop there and I went through a longer process of grieving and recovery, in as much as anyone can. It wasn't just losing Addie, but also the loss of a huge extended family, a way of life and any hope of fitting in and being the same as other children. The expression of any of this grief was impossible in the bewildering silence around death and dying in those days.

The deeper impact only began to unravel after I celebrated my thirty-third birthday, Addie's age at the time of her death. I felt that although I had outlived her and survived, I had somehow reached thirty-three against all the odds. The temptation was to hold everyone I loved very close and protect them in every way possible. I had to learn that

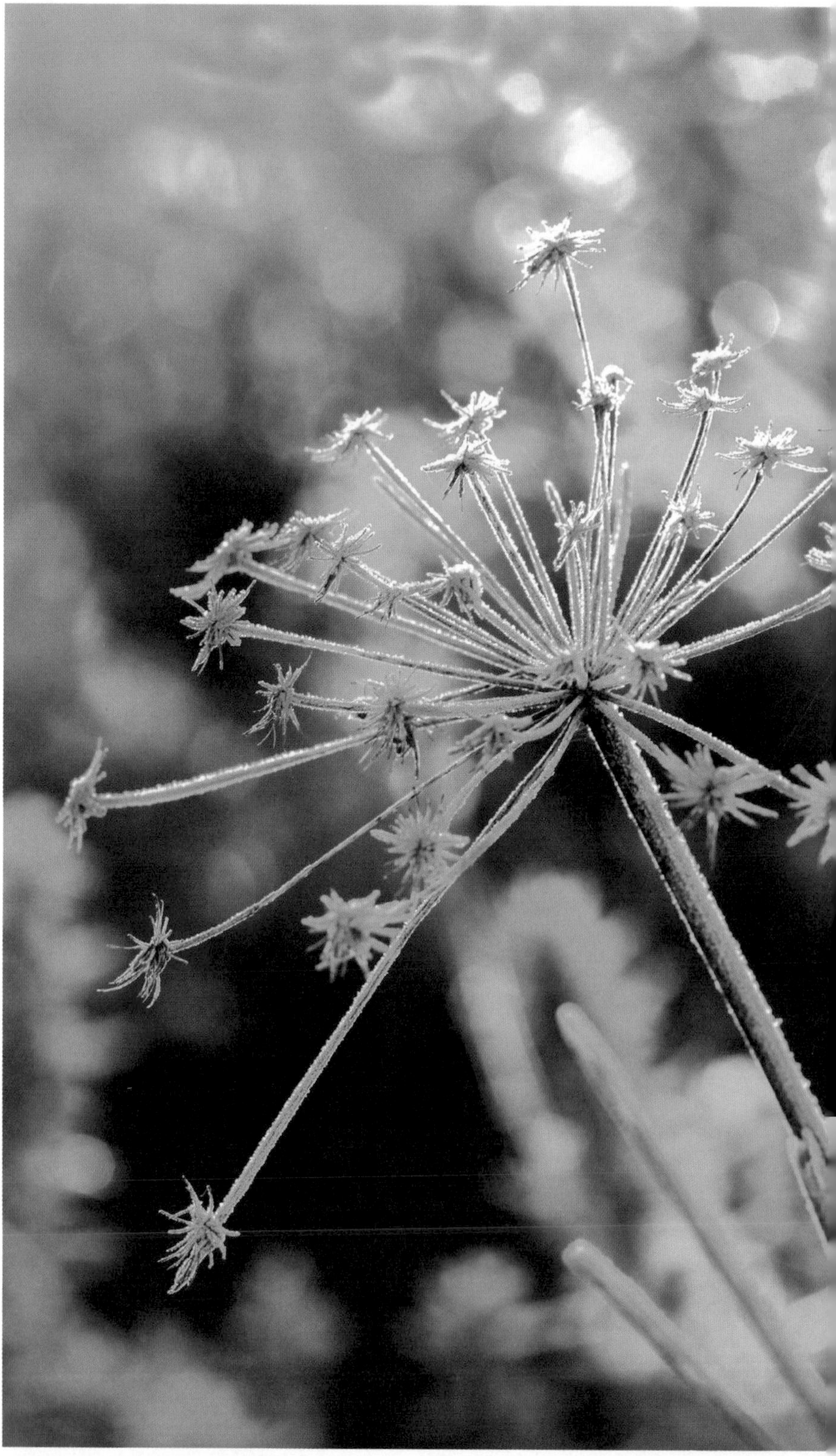

no one has that much control; sometimes you just have to let go.

There was no other way in the end. Pretence, hiding away from the world or tightening up in fear wouldn't bring Addie back, nor would it ease the pain that had followed. So I began to explore counselling and discovered that it was possible to heal from the experiences of my youth. Survivor children who suffer trauma and grief can express and feel it all without losing hope or the chance of happiness.

Yes, there was crying and roaring and thumping pillows. Yes, it was messy and frightening, but at some point in the whole process, it was so rewarding that I decided to study counselling and signed up for a Postgraduate in Integrative Psychotherapy. Exploring the writings of the ones who discovered the value of taking time to relive pain, to feel it, to calm it, helped me to face the fact that 'good enough me' would have to do. I discovered the five stages of grieving as described by psychiatrist Elisabeth Kübler-Ross: denial, anger, bargaining, depression and acceptance. I wasn't that different from other people after all; everyone had particular challenging circumstances to deal with too.

I was nervous about the interview for entry to the course and felt exposed facing a panel of three wise old owls. The questions they asked me are now a blur, but it was intimate and very searching of my life. The more uncomfortable I became, the more my attention was drawn out the window to a familiar group of trees. I stopped looking at the panel and began to answer their questions by finding answers out there in nature.

After a while, one asked, 'Why are you looking out the window so much?'

We all turned to the group of trees that had caught my eye. In that moment, it felt like we were united in sharing the comfort of that rough grove of hawthorn trees laden with the bright red haws of winter. I told them I was nervous and that it calmed me somehow to gaze out there and join in that energy. 'Mother Nature,' one of them remarked to the other two. They both nodded and we returned to the grilling.

That counselling course was perhaps one of the last pieces in the jigsaw. I had been catapulting between the five stages of grief all my life and now wondered if this was finally the acceptance part? But I also learned grief never goes away and lingers in your body and soul, catching you unawares from time to time. A child who tends to hide, who stifles her own needs and works hard to be 'normal', to fit in, can hit road-blocks throughout life. Why do I feel different from other people? Why do I still feel sad? Why do I want to be alone?

It took another fifty years after Addie's death for Dad to finally erect a headstone on her grave. He was elderly and feeble that day as we gathered as a family for the very first time in Deansgrange Cemetery. My inner child held back on the anger and rising confusion over how our childhood grief had been handled and the loneliness of her grave. For Dad, who we all loved so much, we took it in our stride as usual and were 'good girls' for the day. Who knows what's right or wrong in these situations? One thing is certain, I contained that muddled grief so that he got that small bit of closure before he died. Anyone could see that he was soothed by it.

In the end, we each find the solace we need, in our own way. But if I learned anything through my childhood experiences of stifled grief, it's that somehow we can grow to hold dualities as we heal. We can honour the trauma that we have lived, while at the same time thrive and find joy in the world. We can feel the pain of loss when we need to and at the same time have hope for the future. We can talk about the deaths of the ones we love and at the same time be fully present in the exuberance of the living. We can live with heartbreak as well as wonder.

LOVE

One of my sparse memories of Addie happened just before her last Christmas when we were staying in the midlands with her family. I was put to bed early to amuse myself in my parents lonely double bed. It was in the room I had been born in and it was probably the bed I was born in too. There was a massive chest of drawers along one wall of the bedroom, so bored and sleepless, I decided to investigate the drawers.

In one of the drawers I found what I now know were the Christmas presents destined for children of other families staying there for Christmas too. Amongst the array of dinky cars, board games and cuddly toys was an adorable little doll. She had real hair and clothes you could swop, so I immediately took her into bed and changed her outfit many times.

Gradually falling asleep, I forgot to put the doll back and it was discovered by Addie later that night tucked in beside me. 'We won't say a word,' she whispered to me, trying to push the doll back into the opened box.

Next morning, somehow, the other families, aunties and cousins had found out about my misdemeanour and there followed an inquisition.

'Did you root around in the presents and take that doll into your bed?'

I looked at my mother who winked.

'No,' I said. 'No!'

The aunties got more and more angry, called me sneaky and said I was a bold girl for telling such lies. (I'm sure this would have been very obvious to everyone!) I barely remember what I felt except a huge sense of confusion, shock and mortification.

Addie held her nerve. 'You would never tell lies, would you?'

I shook my head, completely out of my depth in this new scenario of lying through your teeth to save your bacon. Her eyes locked mine. The pale-faced girl, with the curly dark hair, my mother had suddenly become a warrior. In her gritty determination to protect me there was a visceral truth. The veracity of love is powerful and lasting.

I wouldn't have Addie in the rest of my life to support or defend me as I grew up, but because of her I know in my bones that even the memory of a tiny sliver of love will make you stronger. I know that mothers don't have to be perfect. And that maybe it's in their darkest moments that mothers teach us how to be strong, especially in the grip of a challenge.

My memories of Addie are few and far between but the feeling, the knowledge of her love is in my every cell. Even the scant memory of love can heal.

SOUL

Soul is a word worth reclaiming from the pristine white soul of Catholic teaching where dark stains of sin would mount up over the years. Soul might be the place where we feel most deeply connected to that which we cannot see, touch, or name. The interior part of ourselves searching for meaning and for whatever some of us name as 'God' and what some call connection.

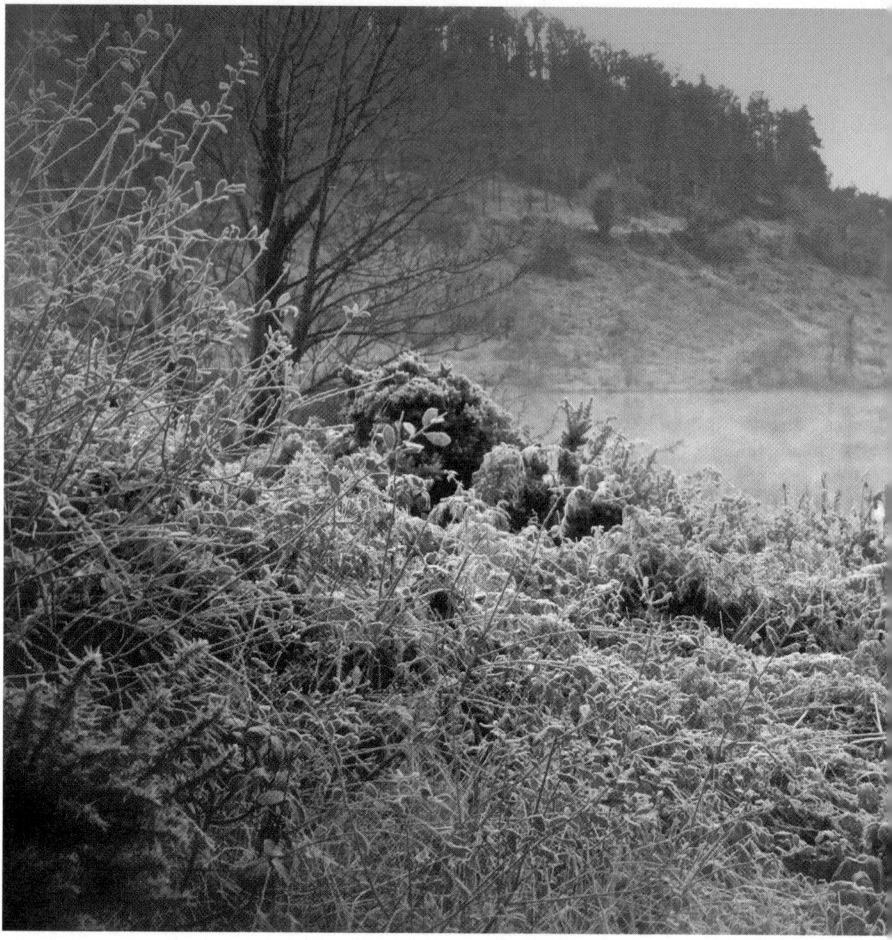

In many cultures the soul is that which exists outside of the physical. There is a view that humans are unique in having a soul, but some theories propose a sentient universe that we are part of: a whole teeming ecosystem of living stars, planets and distant galaxies. That soul is something integrative, something intangible but present in humans, animals and all life forms. The soul's meanderings is where we find solace too.

The ancient Greek philosopher Epicurus first suggested that the soul is found in paying attention to the everyday

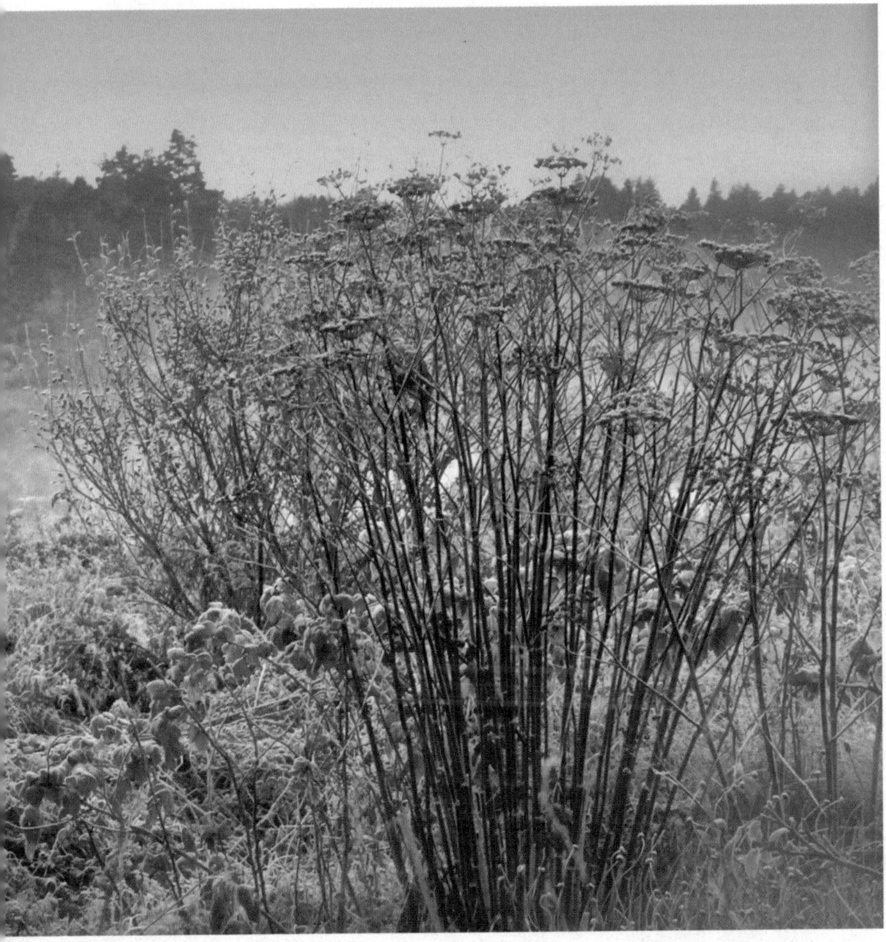

rituals of human life: what we eat and how we prepare it, how we care for our family and friends, in the beauty of our planet, in the loved and the small details of the day, in the ordinary and the commonplace, and in the simple life.

In this simple soul life today, I notice that I am delighted by a silvery winter morning, the opening chords of the music I love and the meditative sound of snow falling lightly on the window pane.

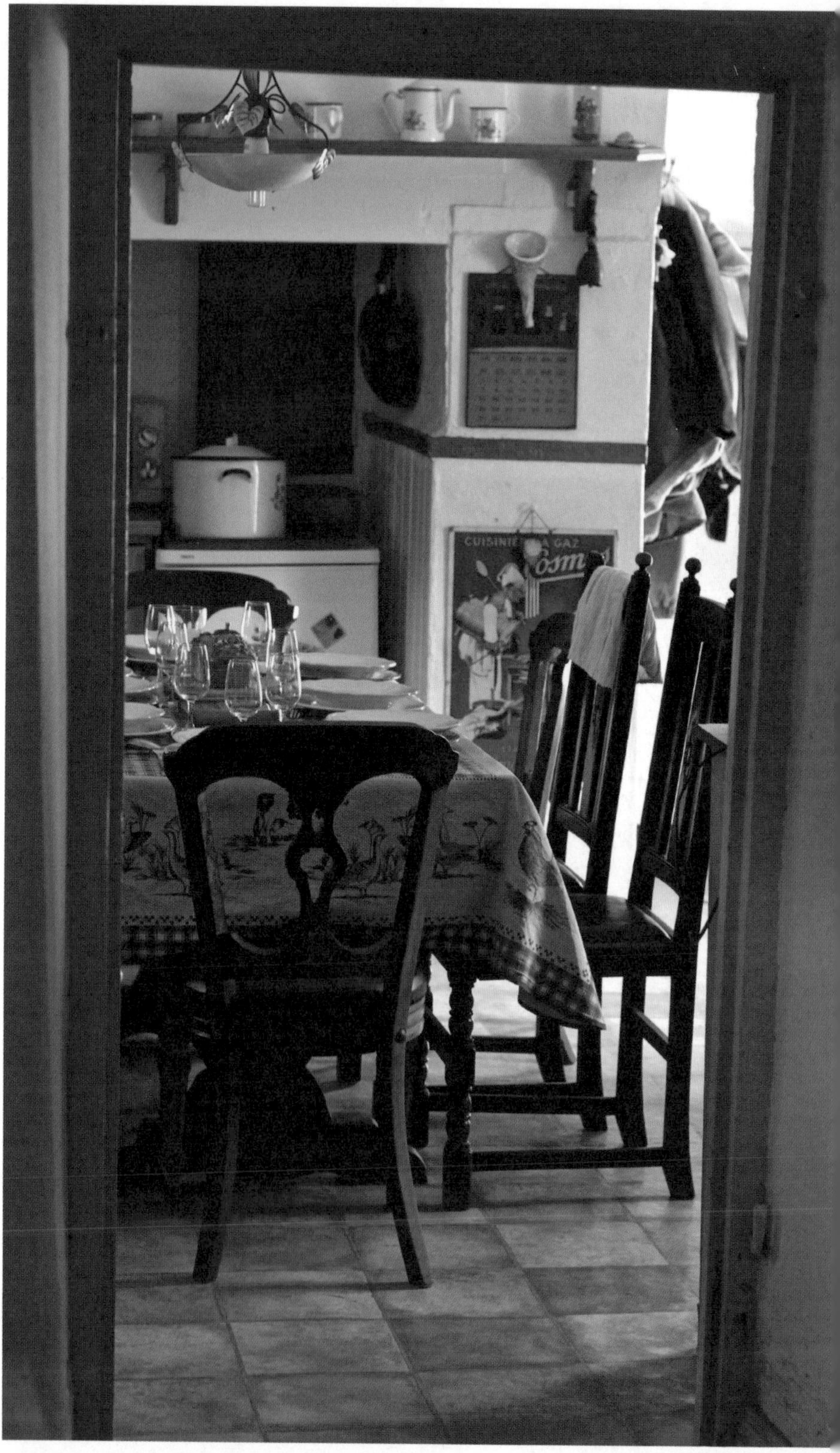

Chapter 15

Map-making

CREATIVITY

All through life I noticed with fascination all the ways that the adults in my family were creative and attentive to making. I always knew the parameters of my own state of flow and Addie's too. Then I began to notice others and the unique ways they manoeuvred themselves into this flow state. How they whistled and tapped their feet, how they smiled or stared into the distance. How my grandfather Dadins, smoked a pipe, silently examining a piece of wood that could become a clock, a table or a pulpit. How adults engrossed in projects didn't notice if we got up to mischief, or that it was past our bedtime. This intense focus on what they were making or doing is a skill I absorbed from each of them.

From my crocheting Grand Aunt Alsie who took up pottery in her eighties to my Nanan who with her talented daughter ran her bustling restaurant until in her nineties. From our exotic Aunt Áine who designed clothes and the interiors of buildings, dressing herself and her mother in colourful silks and fake furs, to Grand Aunt Nora, a seamstress who sewed me a kimono with embroidered sleeves when I was living in the midlands while Addie was ill. From the austere Grand Uncle Martin who combined a church career as a Monsignor with the creative life of a wickedly funny cartoonist, to my cousin's family of visual artists who every year sent us a hand-made Christmas card using a variety of printmaking methods.

All of them influenced how we played and what we learned about a soulful and skilful way of living. Because of them, we children learned how a tea tray could become a sled for barrelling down the stairs. How a garage attached to an ordinary house could become an art gallery selling paintings made by children to casual passers-by. How a set of sliding doors could become curtains on the stage of an opening night.

Everywhere I looked I noticed how people created magic through their own innate creativity. After twenty years of working first as an art teacher, then as a community support worker in our small organisation I finally decided to devote myself full time to creativity, writing and travel.

BECOMING A MAKER

Just before leaving school, a Jesuit priest conducted some sort of psychological suitability tests to find out our skills for

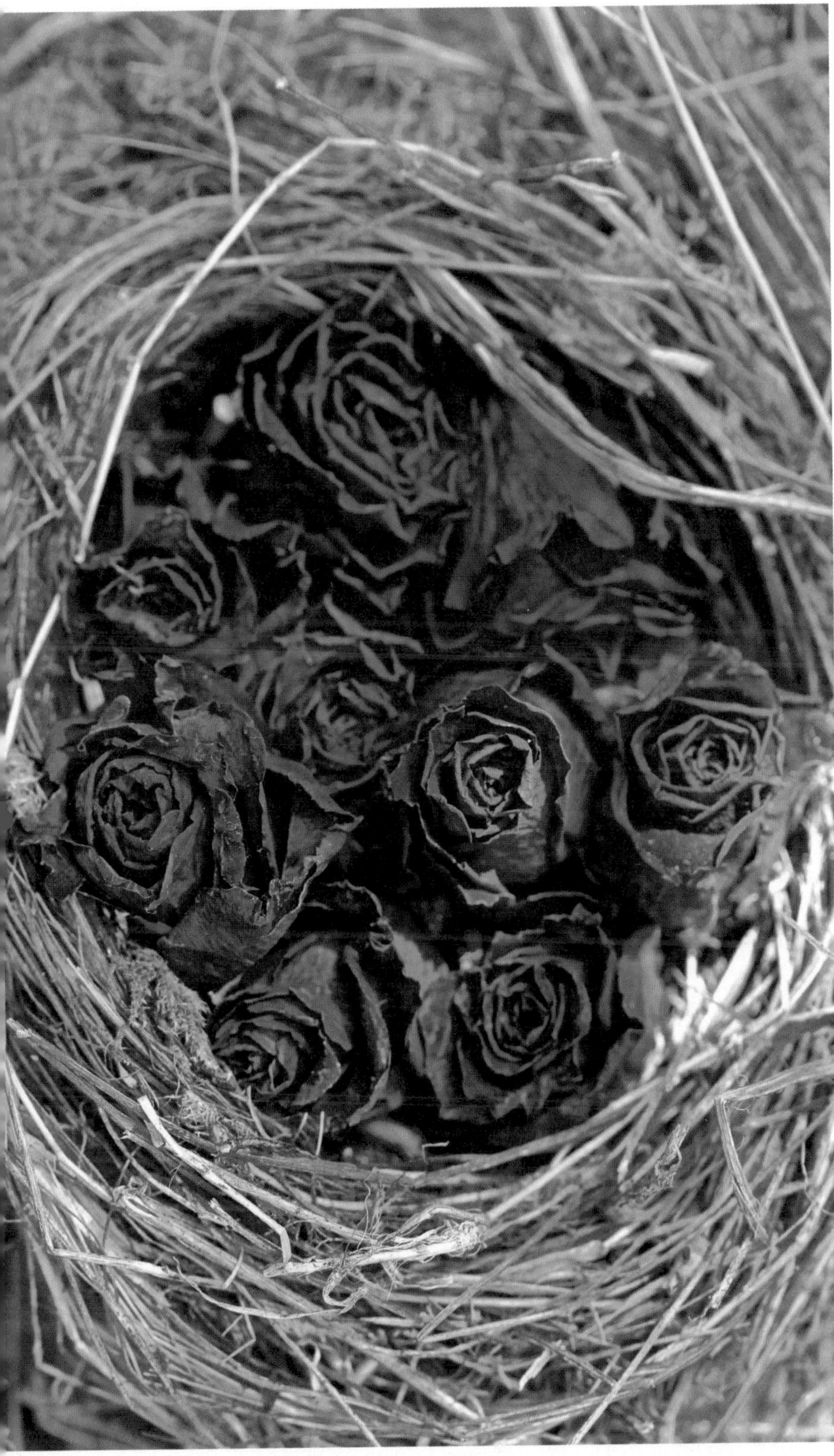

the different career options on offer to girls. After my interview he looked at me over his spectacles and said, 'Mmm, Catherine, don't worry there are lots of careers you could follow, and whatever you do it will be fine. You are creative.' While others were given law or teaching, my results were left like this — vague to say the least.

Here was the invitation to create a life rather than a job. And so it goes. Creative people are required to ebb and flow, to have many hats, many different jobs, many long dark nights of the soul trying to figure out our next steps and how to earn a living. Artists will have to live with rejection, isolation, competition and constantly being told we are 'lucky' while we are asked to contribute to all kinds of projects without any payment.

Making a creative life has its challenges, but also has its joys. The openness and the vulnerability that an artistic inclination fosters can be usefully adapted to all kinds of innovation, problem solving and visioning. Creative types bring light and energy to the mainstream, but most of all are deeply satisfied by an internal landscape of possibility. We may be overcome with ideas, but usually not bored.

Deep in the second winter of the pandemic it became harder to sustain this creative rhythm in the ongoing uncertainty. And yet, at some point in the spaces in between writing and editing, every tiny scrap of paper and board in my space was painted and filed away. There was no projected outcome for these pieces. The creative muse just reassured me that the results were unimportant, and I kept going. It was a desperate attempt to fill the time so as to avoid the oppressive negativity and the gap left by going out.

The result was dozens of tiny paintings brightening the heaviness of ongoing restrictions and isolation. Whether it was making these pieces or just making soup, the pandemic required a lot of much deeper digging to get through the day.

VERY LONG WALKS

A very long walk is surely going to be one where anything that can go wrong will go wrong. There will be tiredness and thirst along the way. Someone is sure to get 'hangry' for the want of a meal. There will be misunderstandings and one of us will probably read the map the wrong way up or be interrupted by the need to turn back for something.

A very, very long walk requires pacing and good humour. You need to have lots to talk about and also know when it's best to be silent. Then again, there's no point in setting out with someone who will always agree with you. Difference is the seasoning on the meal, the magic dust that makes conversation sparkle. On the other hand, it is also a recipe for conflict.

These days, almost fifty years since we first met, myself and my Right-Hand Man have found a peaceful tempo on the long walk. Instead of a linear walk to a destination we seem to be on a rambling spiral path. We go out, around and back the way on this path. We revisit the past, but selectively and carefully. We avoid bumping into each other, cramping each other's style or getting hassled about the right route or which way to turn.

Something we always laugh about is that when we are travelling together, which we have done a lot, our individual preferences can cause havoc when they are let loose. We once drove around a roundabout in France, round and around, because we were arguing about which exit we should take. My side of the argument was that we should have figured this out before we found ourselves driving around and around. His argument was that we needed to take any bloody random exit or we would be on the roundabout forever. You see the dilemma.

An introvert like me who is cautious and wants to fade into the background can be very challenged by an extrovert who is curious about everything and is at ease with taking risks. Having said that, I have had wonderful adventures that would have been impossible on my own as I would surely have stayed in my shell in order to take the safe option. I think, on the other hand, my reflective side brings an element of forward-thinking to the party, and I will always try to make at least the outline of a plan that we can follow when we hit the road out of here.

We are, neither of us, very conventional, I suppose, but that has made the long walk together a bit easier as we allow for our quirkiness and the odd surprise. Nothing else could possibly work! As Belgian psychotherapist Ester Perrel says, relationships are best navigated as 'a meeting of two solitudes'. Never as a 'two becoming one'! Perhaps my best role models for two solitudes were my grandparents, one staring quietly at a piece of wood while the other served up roast beef to chatty Americans in her restaurant. And yet, always side by side.

DOWN THE TRACK

A precious walk is one on a track made for two, or more. Having had to walk alone in those early days of working from home, I enjoy more than ever sharing a walk with anyone who joins me along the way. My oldest pals, with their creaky joints and diverse perspectives on life, make these simple walks solace and a balm.

We often begin with what Dublin writer Maeve Binchy christened the 'organ recital'. This is the updating section

of the session. How is your bad back? Did you get your blood results? Are you still waiting for that appointment? The organ recital gives each of us time to share the latest on health matters. Sometimes we just laugh and skip to the chase, acknowledging that yes the bad back is still there, the wonky hip is still wonky, the high blood pressure is still high!

We have walked with each other through thick and thin. The early years of marriage and children, the separations and divorces, the teenage angst of the next generation throwing all our expectations up in the air. We have lost friends and we have found new friends. Now we grow old and share notes. But mostly we enjoy the coffee and chat when we finally sit down outside one of our local cafés on the prom and stare into Tramore Bay with all the other earthlings who appreciate such moments.

PILGRIMS

Much as travel is a solace and a joy, during the pandemic we were confined to home more than ever. Setting out and beginning again took on new connotations. During the second winter of the virus, we were anxious to travel again. But for many, the decision of which way to turn was a virtual one.

There was a lot of mooching through maps during the wintertime hibernation. As we travel mostly by ferry, the map research is of ferry crossings all over Europe, which at this stage of our lives is our main destination. I never tire of crossing the threshold of our home into the new adventure that will be ahead: leaving, crossing the sea, arriving, circling and returning.

Winter research is about collecting possibilities. The main decision will be where the ports of departure and entry will be. Ireland being an island requires a sea crossing no matter what country you are going to. Having managed to fly to far-flung places for many years we are now very happy to wander around our own beautiful island or to take one of these ferries.

There is a special pleasure in arriving in the low-key working ports around Europe – like arriving in Roscoff, moving very slowly through the landscape of the Bay of La Manche.

As we travel just a few kilometres from one place to the next, we wonder, 'Can it get any better?' It always does. All along the way, we will have to choose left or right, north or

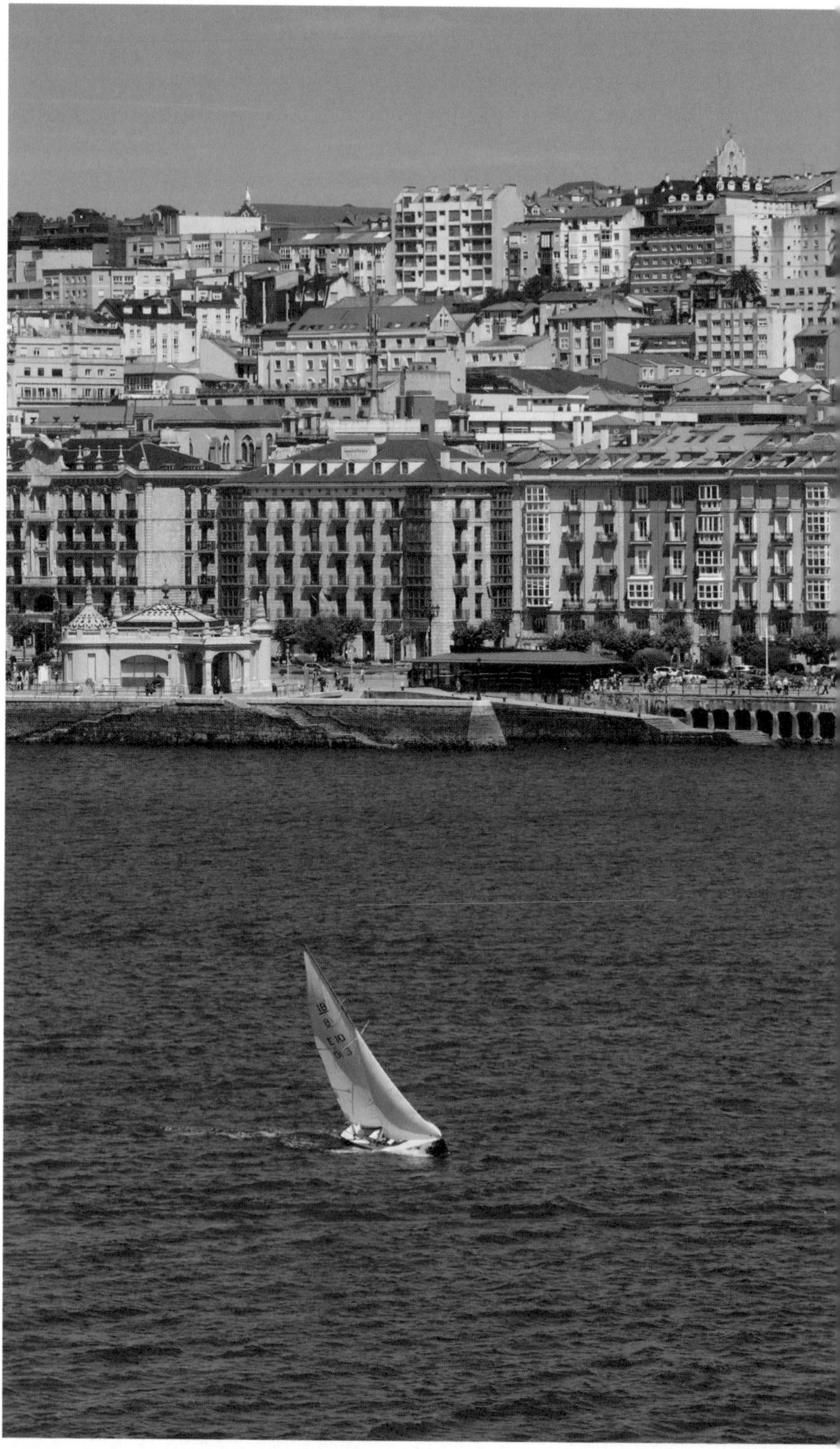

south, east or west. We will wake up some morning and just know that our direction will be this or that due to weather, or the romance of a name on the map or maybe just a hunch.

On arrival anywhere the usual overenthusiasm for colour and textures will have my eyes on high alert, snapping everything that moves. Sometimes I will have a lump in my throat at the beauty of these arrivals in new places.

Like when we spent our first night in Brittany in the middle of a coastal field on L'île Callot, an island cut off from the mainland at high tide. Where, on waking early the next morning, a congregation of white egrets landed on the trees above our heads. Or when arriving in Kardamili in the Peloponnese we found that the window of our tavern room opened up onto a sunny harbour. Here you could almost dive into the deep blue sea from your bed. How I was hugged and kissed because I complimented a cook on her aubergine pie and because I tried to understand the recipe she shared in very fast Greek — the dance of sign language and the enthusiasm for connecting making that 'conversation' possible.

Or maybe we will arrive again in northern Spain, where the ferry from Cork docks right in the centre of the city of Santander. As it pulls into the quay, daily strollers are promenading, relaxing on the local beaches or marvelling at the contemporary architecture of the art gallery on the waterfront. One minute you are on a huge ship docking carefully, and the next you are photographing a Spanish heron and drinking coffee in a cafe on the prom.

Where to next? We will wonder sleepily over breakfast. Maybe a hop, skip and jump from Comillas, Llanes, Ribadesella, Lastres, Luanco to Cudillero? A meander through the lush and green fishing villages clinging to the sides of cliffs or perhaps a trip through the mountain range, often snow-covered, separating northern Spain from the rest of the mainland.

Or we could end up heading south through wild broom-filled and heather-scented picnic spots, mountain passes, tunnels and hairpin bends until we reach Zamora – all hot and summery. Or further still, down towards the Douro Valley, through miles of vineyards, some more than two thousand years old. At Lamego in northern Portugal we could climb the 675 steps to the Santuario Nossa Senhora dos Remedios in the belting sun, or sample the local port, a blend of brandy and wine, developed to preserve the wine on long sea crossings.

On our travels we have encountered other pilgrims walking and crossing inhospitable lands and waters to reach safety after turmoil and wars in their own countries. Some have even reached Ireland where they can finally lay their heads down and rest. Meeting them along the way, living in tents, praying for comfort and sanctuary is to be confronted with devastating pain. These courageous pilgrims, forced to leave their homes behind, have an aching need for solace, one which we can all relate to. In the exhausted but elated crowd in front of the Cathedral of Santiago de Compostela, I wonder where all the displaced of the world will finally find the end of their Camino.

Whether it's on the open road or just outside the back door, myself and my Right-Hand Man will continue to put one foot in front of the other as do all the others that we meet along the way.

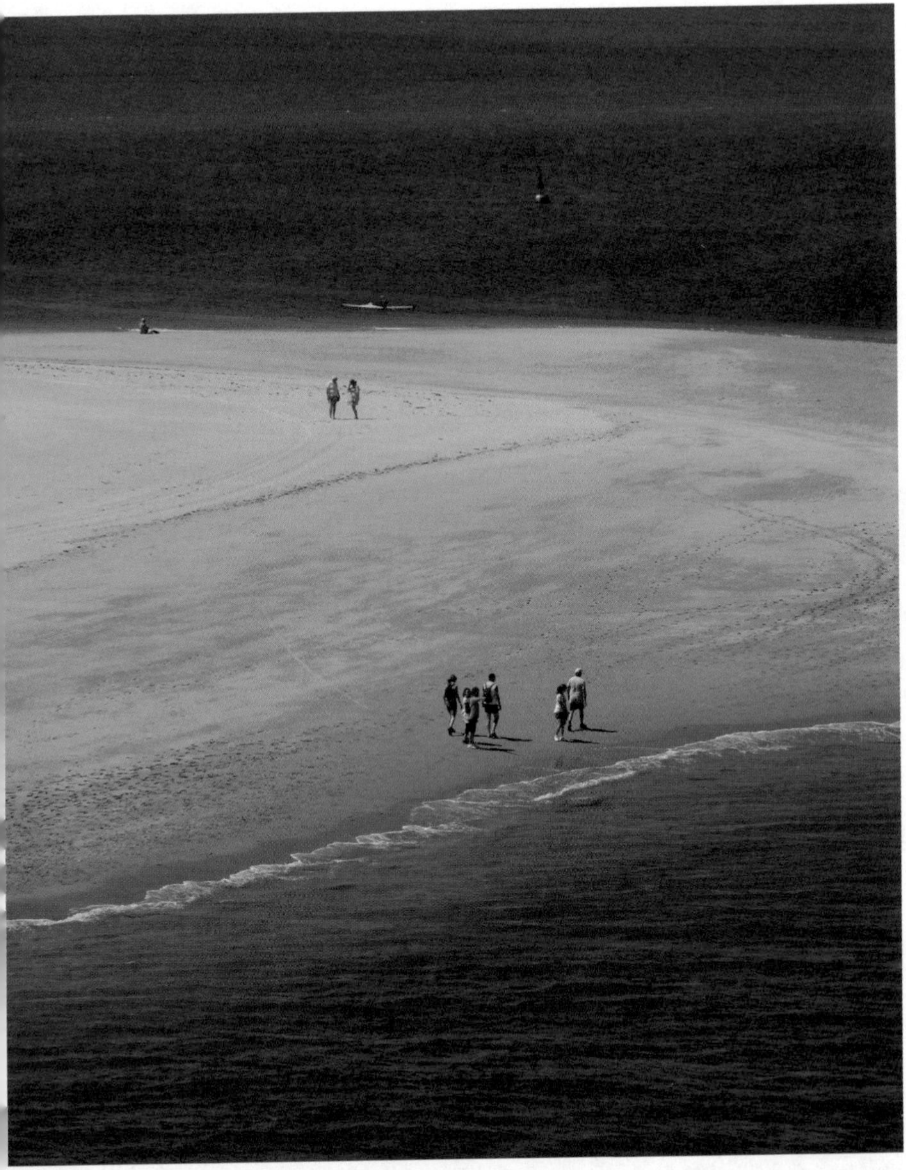

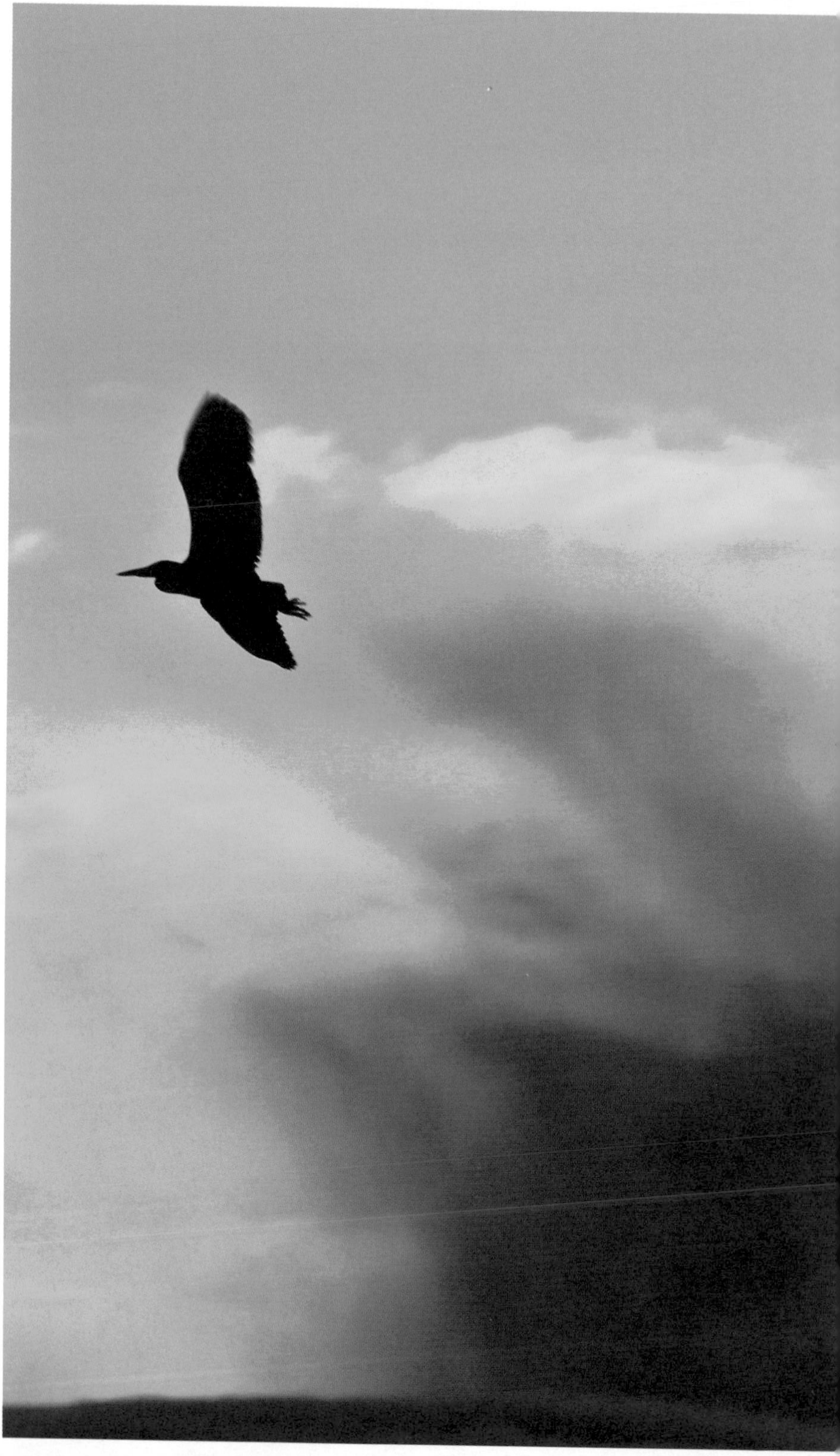

Chapter 16

Beginning again
and again

Light returns

As the pandemic drags on and on, it is harder to find resilience in the greyness of winter. In our family alone we have lost our eldest member and one of our very youngest. In my small circle of friends, a dear artistic soul has just gone too. At times the grief is overwhelming.

I have become the age of the adults who were around me when Addie died. I feel a similar ambivalence of, on the one hand, going deeply into the sadness and, at the same time, looking out to the horizon and carrying on. If I've learned anything it is that we need to talk about our grief, our dead loved ones and our pain. I try to say the words, dying, death, dead. I try to allow the sadness and the mystery to breathe. The Cailleach in me knows how to, but I am still learning even though time is short.

Some of my oldest buddies make me laugh as we reminisce and talk food on the beach. I light candles, ramble the tracks and feed the birds. The stillness of a cold winter morning is a steady presence.

Light gradually returns after the winter solstice. As the evenings lengthen, I begin to look forward to spring again when the first swallows fly in low over the lake. Then I will hear the first cuckoo who arrives here from Africa every April and can be heard calling in the distance, presumably making mischief in the forest beyond. There is solace in that light even in the intensity of sadness.

MAKING NATURE OUR OWN

I didn't learn about farming, plants or animals as a child so nothing could have prepared me for moving to the wilds of rural Ireland and being immersed in Mother Nature. It is never too late to discover and explore the complexity of the natural world. There is no 'right' way to connect with nature, but I will put my hands up now and admit that as a result of coming to it all so late in life, with my inner child in tow, I am very much a 'romantic' as regards my relationship to her.

It was when I read a nature writer apologising for using the term 'Mother Nature' that I found myself rebelling. It isn't lost on me that my early childhood connection to the natural world and the space created by Addie has transferred

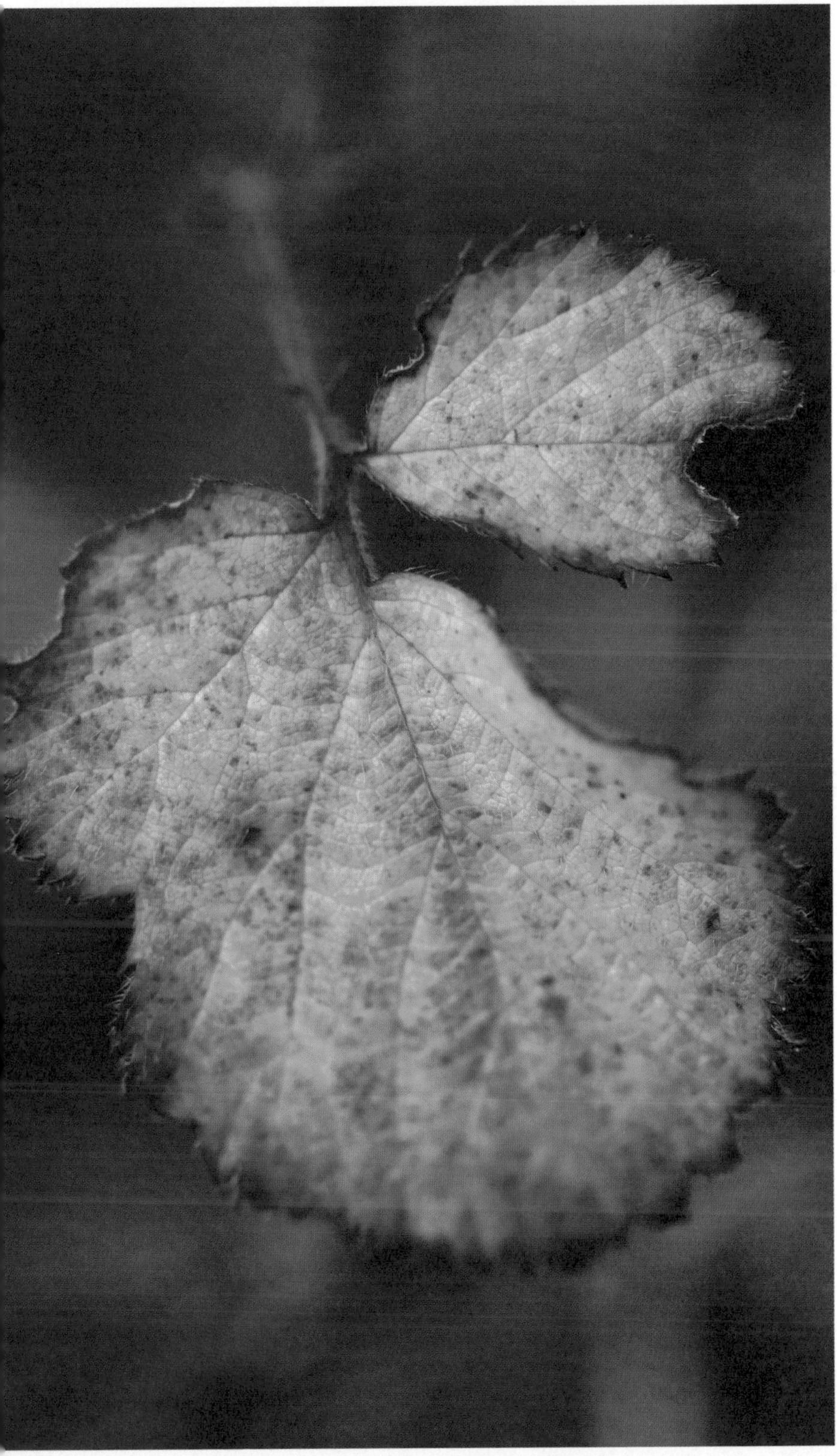

onto my current relationship with this small patch around me. Mother Earth and my own experience of nurturing merge into the wonder of it all.

I am not an ecologist, a biologist or a botanist. I relate with heart rather than head. It's a quirk of artistic training that as artist Paul Klee said, 'One eye sees and the other feels.' It is an intuitive approach rather than a scientific one. Too much Latin is still hard to bear after years of those dull secondary-school textbooks and as I get older I find it even harder to retain the many names of wildflowers for example. It's enough for me to love what I see, name what I know and find out what I don't.

I also tend to relate to things visually rather than verbally. Once I have photographed something, it will remain in my memory forever and allow me to review the details of tracks and trails that I have seen with my camera. Even the daily practice of photography itself is a kind of meditation in my life rather than any other kind of aspiration. With my eyesight fading, there is great craic to be had from the big screen images of bugs and beetles that I had no idea were even present on a pretty flower when I clicked the shutter.

My early curiosity began with textures, shapes and colours in nature rather than species names or any scientific enquiry. Through this training of my eye, I have found that there is a harmony between beauty and caring, between art and nature. Whatever way we find to connect with the peace and beauty of the wild is good enough.

There's no need to sweat about the naming of things or

the particular way anyone else relates to nature. We are all in our own unique relationship with the world and we bring our own meaning to it. And mine is a simple-minded version, I'm not one to lecture anyone. Exploring and enjoying the living world is for absolutely everyone.

Jane Goodall, the primatologist, was initially excited by the relationships she could build with the 'personalities' she observed in animals, rather than what she refers to as cold and academic research. She was criticised for giving animals names, for suggesting they were individuals, for re-writing the methodologies of studying and observing nature. In the end, her innovations and her contributions struck a chord with new generations of scientists and explorers. Her unusual approach was eventually validated.

You will see things in your way too. There is no ideal or any hierarchy when it comes to developing connections to the vast diversity of the world. So in spite of science and rational theory, the pre-Christian idea of the sacred feminine captivates me more than the coldness of the word 'environment'. The idea that there is a maternal force at work in nature and the soft feminine movement of the land is something I feel, rather than know.

SOLASTALGIA

There are two high viewing points on the walking trails near my home. One faces east, looking out over the old reservoir, down to the town of Tramore and the expanse of the bay.

The other faces west over the lake, stretching out over the valley all the way to the Comeraghs and Helvic Head.

Each of these promontories requires an uphill stroll. To the east through a dark forest, to the west up a rocky hillside. These places are where I go to drink in the beauty of the sky and to lift my spirits.

I take it all in, reflecting on how we are the luckiest, most blessed people on the planet right now. The privilege that we in the developed world experience is incredible: the peace in Ireland after so many years of struggle, the gradual inclusion of women who have been marginalised, the abundance. Thanks to the hard work of generations, we are without doubt living through a glorious epoch on many levels.

Recently I found a new word 'solastalgia' meaning being emotional or distressed about the loss of nature. So while solace is finding peace and balm in nature, solastalgia is feeling sad at the threat of losing it. Solastalgia captures something that is rising in some of us. A feeling that the planet is teetering on another edge between hope and devastation.

I increasingly feel solastalgia as I scan the valley of farmland below. Everywhere I look is a reminder of something I am struggling to name. What is the word for where the untouched willow woods and wetlands around us have been drained and sprayed and only small pockets remain? How can I communicate about the intense clearing of vegetation, scrub, trees, wildlife flora and fauna? Does it matter that the greenest grass in Ireland is forced and fake?

I am remembering the feeling of panic the day the diggers moved into the meadows around the lake. I called the local council begging them to visit the site and to protect it as far as possible. In fairness to them they insisted that thirty metres of land on its shores were to be untouched. Every year I remain grateful to our neighbouring farmers that this has been adhered to. This beautiful strip of land is all that is left of the original wetland of hazels and purple loosestrife that I had grown to know so well.

As I look out on this small patch of Ireland, with the sun setting behind the mountains, it must be solastalgia that I am feeling as I mourn the dramatic decrease in small animals and wildflowers. I remember the day twenty years ago when I found a star-shaped, maroon-coloured flower down amongst the hazels — now gone. I went searching for its name, the Marsh Cinquefoil, nowhere to be found around here now. Or the cold morning when I photographed the icy winter patterns on a huge meadow of knapweed — now turned into rye grass for grazing. Or the hundreds of dancing butterflies that used to transform the ditches — now very much in decline. After years of spraying and fertilising, there are fewer hares, rabbits, foxes, badgers, slugs, snails, beetles, spiders, worms, caterpillars and ladybirds.

I struggle to find the words, or to know what might unlock the better instinct of earthlings to give more protection and safeguarding to Mother Earth and ultimately to our own human survival. I fail to find the words that might make a difference, over and over again. There is a loneliness to solastalgia and a constant search for hope.

PATCHWORK

I search for clues as to how we earthlings and our planet might thrive together in the future. Perhaps a combination of technology and traditional practices will bring about the best results? I have lived through the rallying around of local communities and have seen how positive change can be achieved by working together. Surely we will find ways of innovating and adapting as we always have. Our intelligence and humanity will rise up to get us through the problems we now face?

Just as love heals us in our human lives, so love of our earthly home could protect our future more than anything else. I imagine that from urban gardens, to the window-sills of flat dwellers and from my couple of wild acres to the

farmland hectares of the professionals, each of us has a role to play in that. There are millions of us falling in love with gardens, community green areas, wild nature, sea swimming and growing our own. By linking up all our love of green spaces and our critical headspaces we could create a messy patchwork quilt of biodiversity and happy earthlings.

We could transform how we care and tend the earth we so depend on. We could plant vegetables amongst the flowers, and herbs and blossoming fruit trees amongst the neat urban hedges. Our city streets could be lined with nut trees and berries; schools and hospitals could be built in the middle of forests or on lush riversides instead of in concrete wastelands. We don't have to wait for someone else to do it. Individuals and communities can make a difference and that's where all my hopes are pinned for now.

We don't have to know it all; it doesn't have to be perfect.

We just have to allow in some extra discombobulation, follow our caring instincts and learn as much as we can about how to live a simpler life. Maybe I need to come up with better answers, but for now this is where I find my solace when thinking about the future of our living world.

Breathe easy

Winter provides breathing space. We slow down, stay warm and reflect. We prepare for scattering seeds as the ground opens again to the spring. Soon the days will warm and the butterflies and insects will return to the creeping thistle flowers they love so much. Already the evenings are brighter and buds are emerging on the hedgerows. From now on the golden gorse blooms profusely

Each one of us, falling in love with our own place and the small beings that we share our planet with, is our hope for the future. If the spiders on the trees around us are spinning, alive and healthy, then probably so are we. If the ditches are overflowing with wildflowers and bees, then our apple trees will continue to produce delicious fruit. If the habitats and wild areas are protected, then the joy and solace we experience in the web of life can be preserved. Spring will come after winter, morning comes after the night, and we will begin again and again.

As time goes on the Cailleach and the inner child in me have no conflict. Each one allows the other space – the inner child holding out for the magic and beauty around us, the

Cailleach exerting the determination to stand our ground as diverse and united earthlings. On a late winter's day, just as I was pinning all my hopes on spring, a young hare jogged past me. In January they begin to breed again and as they often leave a newborn leveret here in the wild garden I wondered if we might be in luck again. Then this morning there she was, the tiniest leveret I have ever seen nibbling at the succulents growing between the stones outside the kitchen window. She will grow taller and soon a shapeshifting Irish hare will sit outside the kitchen window, meditate on her own reflection and I will be still and full of wonder.

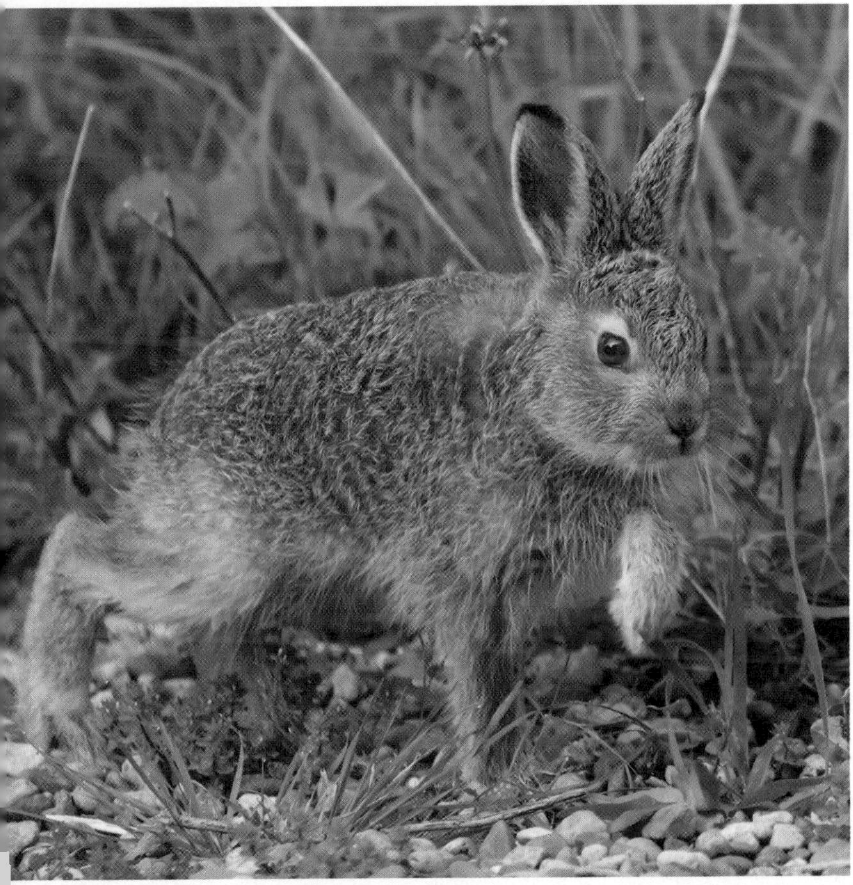

The poets

Róisín Sheehy is a poet, playwright and broadcaster. *Líomóidí's Rúbarb,* her first poetry collection, was published by Coiscéim in 2021. Her debut play *Snámh na Saoirse* was awarded a Stewart Parker/BBC Northern Ireland award. Róisín's second play *An Bhean a Saolaíodh ar Charraig* was awarded an Oireachtas na Samhna award. Her poetry has been published in various journals, such as *Poetry Ireland Review, Irish Pages*, and *Comhar*. Róisín is invigorated by dance. She recently moved inland from the broad waves of Tramore to the quieter waters of the River Nore in Thomastown.

The link for the book *Líomóidí's Rúbarb*: https://www.siopaleabhar.com/tairge/liomoidi-agus-rubarb/

Mary Frances Ryan has been editor of Waterford's award-winning local newspaper the *Waterford News & Star* for more than thirteen years. She has built a team of exceptional journalists, who regularly investigate and break stories of national significance. One of the country's youngest female editors when she took up the role aged thirty, Mary Frances started her career in *The Wexford Echo* stable of newspapers. She graduated from UCD, with a BA (Hons) in English and History, and completed her Masters in Journalism at DIT. The north-Wexford native lives in New Ross with her two children. Away from work, she writes poetry and is a regular contributor to the Spokes Open Mic group in Waterford city. After that, you're most likely to find her hiking the Blackstairs Mountains or exploring the Hook peninsula, which inspired the poem that is featured in this book.

Joanne McCarthy writes bilingually, in English and Irish, in Waterford. Her work is published and anthologised in *Poetry Ireland Review*, *The Stinging Fly*, *Irish Independent New Irish Writing*, *Hold Open the Door: The Ireland Chair of Poetry Anthology*, *The Honest Ulsterman*, *The Stony Thursday Book*, *Comhar*, *Aneas*, *Splonk* and elsewhere. In 2021, her poetry was highly commended at the Desmond O'Grady International Poetry Competition; she placed second in the Cathal Buí Poetry Competition and was a John Hewitt International Summer School bursary recipient. She is co-founder and co-editor of the literary journal *The Waxed Lemon*.